POETRY COMPETITION

GREAT MINDS

Your World...Your Future...YOUR WORDS

From Birmingham

Edited by Steve Twelvetree

# Young**Writers**

First published in Great Britain in 2005 by:
Young Writers
Remus House
Coltsfoot Drive
Peterborough
PE2 9JX
Telephone: 01733 890066
Website: www.youngwriters.co.uk

SB ISBN 1 84460 712 7

Foreword

This year, the Young Writers' 'Great Minds' competition proudly presents a showcase of the best poetic talent selected from over 40,000 up-and-coming writers nationwide.

Young Writers was established in 1991 to promote the reading and writing of poetry within schools and to the youth of today. Our books nurture and inspire confidence in the ability of young writers and provide a snapshot of poems written in schools and at home by budding poets of the future.

The thought, effort, imagination and hard work put into each poem impressed us all and the task of selecting poems was a difficult but nevertheless enjoyable experience.

We hope you are as pleased as we are with the final selection and that you and your family continue to be entertained with *Great Minds From Birmingham* for many years to come.

Contents

Hodge Hill School

Jay Droch (13)	85
Leeanne Jade Davis (12)	85
Stephanie Bryant (12)	86
Chloe Davies (12)	86
Francesca Cox (13)	87
Haaris Gozal (11)	87
Ashleigh Pickering (12)	88
Daryll Lewis (14)	88
Dwayne Manning (12)	89
Sam Smith	89
Jake McDermott (12)	90
Rebecca Tredaway (12)	90
Michelle Bailey (14)	91
Stephen Harrison (12)	91
Rachel Ellen (13)	92
Rosie Middleton (13)	92
Kamaara Natanya Mehay (13)	93
Katie Woodhall (13)	93
Sam Smith (13)	94
Daniel Prosser (13)	94
Luke Vernon (13)	95
Naomi Hylton (13)	95
Shahzan Zafar (14)	96
Limara Dearn (12)	96
Fawn Roberts-Robinson (13)	97
Kerry Bridgewater (15)	98
Zoe Bond (14)	99
Ashley Cottrill (14)	100
Kellie Cockerill (14)	101
Kristina Hemmings (14)	102
Ashley Christopher (14)	103
Blaine Lindsay (14)	104
Spencer Mayes (14)	105
Grace Sparkes (14)	106
Carly Jones (14)	106
Gary Taylor (13)	107
Zahid Shaffique (11)	107
Danielle Westwood (11)	108
James Pate (11)	108
Bianca V Bernard (12)	109

King Edward VI Five Ways School

Kingsbury School

Park Hall School

Kurt Andrews (13)   191
Grace Harding (13)   191
Caroline Bolding (12)   192
Louise Winston (13)   192
Emily Tsontilis (13)   193
Megan Heath (11)   193
Emma Stokes (14)   194
Bethany Stevens (11)   194
Chloe Waplington (11)   195
Laura Solly (13)   195
Matthew Jacques (13)   196
Lauren Sweeney (11)   196
Thomas Roff (12)   197
Rachael Thompson (13)   197
Jade Walker (12)   198
Vicky Burbidge (15)   198
Stephen Oakley (12)   198
Stacey Browne (14)   199
Jordan Wheeler (12)   199
Catherine Elliot (12)   200
Ashley Robinson (13)   200
Joshua Crawley (12)   201
Gemma Honey (11)   201
Kristian Bow (12)   202

Priestley Smith School
Haroon Rashid (12)   202
Matthew Horspool (12)   203
Robana Begum (12)   203
Aneeba Ahmed (13)   204

St Albans CE School, Highgate
Muna Abraham (11)   204
Anisa Abdou (11)   205
Charlene O'Donnell (11)   205
Marcia Miles (11)   206

Stockland Green School
Nicole Bradley (12)   206
Kirsty Johnson (12)   207
Emma Kigonya (11)   207

The Poems

The Pointless War

The horses' feet gallop across sodden lands,
They reach their destinations and dismount,
In the distance the men hear the guns,
Will they get out alive?

Cannons roar out like a bullet to the brain,
The men run forward in vain.
The soldiers watch as their friends fall around them.
Will it happen to them?

As the bullets spear the soldier's chest,
The pain inside him is released with anger,
Soldiers help him to his feet but his legs give in,
He is left there, blood seeping through his dirty clothes,
He knows his time has come.

Has the war been won?

Rebecca Johnson (13)
Edgbaston High School

Christmas Holiday

Snowflakes falling on the ground,
Friends and family coming round.

Shorter days and longer nights,
Children having snowball fights.

Presents arrive every day,
While we hope Santa's on his way.

Ice skating and sledging is so much fun,
Apart from when you fall on your bum!

Christmas Day, time to rest,
Of all the days, this is the best!

Laura Grindulis (13)
Edgbaston High School

A Winter's Morning

The cold air touches my cheeks
as I wake from the long night
and open my sleepy eyes
to another winter's morning.

I open my curtains with a shiver
and stare at the carpet of snow
and look forward to a wintry walk to school
filled with snow fights and snowmen.

I drag my feet down the stairs
and enter the dining room,
the smell of warm porridge greets me
as I sit down at the table.

I wrap up warmly in my coat, hat and scarf
and hurry out the frozen door
leaving footsteps as I go
and watch my breath flow away.

Sophie Francis-Cansfield (12)
Edgbaston High School

On The 31st of October

Witches fly high in the sky.
The moon is full and shines so bright.
Black cats are out and pumpkins lit.
All on the 31st of October.

Scary masks and face paint,
Trick or treating with your mates
In the dark of the night.
All on the 31st of October.

Having fun and celebrating.
Eating sweets and party food.
Going to bed really spooked.
All on the 31st of October.

Hannah Bevins (13)
Edgbaston High School

A Day In The Life Of . . .

My teacher strides into class on Monday
We're all wishing it was still a Sunday.
On the desk, a detention slip
And we're all thinking,
He's going to flip!
'Now come on 9C,
We are going to be the best,
Never mind the rest!'
We all nod, concealing smiles
He wants us to try all the while.
Hurrying down to assembly,
But not single file like we're meant to be!
Whispering and giggling, some people fiddling
With scrunchies and skirts,
Dishing the dirt.
Late for first lesson, but waiting for break,
Rushing to lunch - what a mistake!
Custard with skin, straight in the bin,
Then off down the field while our lunch congeals.
Afternoon school, no playing the fool,
We now need to focus, no time for jokers.
It's time to go home, get out your phone,
Ring up your mum and yell, 'When will you come?'
The end of the day - the best time for me,
We are the best, we are 9C!

Maya Tankaria (13)
Edgbaston High School

Gracefully

Gracefully a ballerina glides in the air.
Gracefully I jump from chair to chair.
Gracefully I read a prayer.
Gracefully I sit and stare.
Gracefully I float into my bed.
Gracefully dreams swim into my head.

Zaynah Chishti (11)
Edgbaston High School

If

(Based on 'If' by Rudyard Kipling)

If you can get older and keep your fashion sense
And resist mutton dressed as lamb,
If you can talk about others behind their backs
But make allowance for their talking too,
If you can meet with Trinny and Susannah
And treat those two impostors just the same,
If you can walk and dance in heels
And miss every crack in the pavement,
If you can dream of shoes - and not make dreams your master
If you can think of boys - and not make thoughts your aim,
If you can bear to hear the truth you've spoken
Twisted by girls to make a trap for friends,
Or watch the wardrobe you've given your life to, go out of fashion,
And stoop to build it up with worn-out tools,
If you can multitask, as only we can do
While men struggle around you,
If you can fill the unforgiving minute
With sixty seconds' worth of gossip
Yours is the Earth and everything that's in it,
And what is more - you'll be a woman, my daughter!

Charlotte Dean (13)
Edgbaston High School

Smiles

Some people walk around with a large smiley grin,
Those sort of people have a dimply chin,

In church was a man walking down the aisle,
On his face was a great, big, happy smile,

On weekdays when my mum goes to work,
There's a horrible man who gives her a smirk,

When I'm very happy, I seem to gleam,
A very big, smiley, jolly beam!

Elizabeth Hartley (13)
Edgbaston High School

A Recipe For A Poem

Preheat the oven at gas mark five,
And when the blue flame's lit,
Weigh out eight ounces of metaphors,
And mix with a teaspoon of wit.

Now melt a spoon of alliteration,
Until smooth and soft,
Rub in a handful of adjectives,
When you've turned the gas ring off.

Stir the two lots of ingredients,
With some similes for good measure,
Pour the mixture into a baking tin,
And add puns at your pleasure.

The mixture should now be creamy,
So leave to set for twenty minutes,
Then cut into squares (called verses),
And your poem's nearly finished.

Sprinkle the slices with thought,
And, on a baking tray,
Put into the oven for half an hour,
And serve to your audience straightaway!

Bethan Jones (12)
Edgbaston High School

My Family

Dad is busy rushing round,
While Mum picks up toys off the ground.

My brother, he plays cricket,
His aim is to hit a wicket.

My sister is a pain,
She can sometimes act insane.

My baby brother is two years old,
And now he's ill with a cold.

Anisah Shoaib (14)
Edgbaston High School

A Snowflake's Journey

The perfect little star,
Born so high,
With a billion others,
In the grey winter sky.

Dreamily it starts drifting,
Heading towards the ground,
Soaring now - it's going too fast,
Look! It's touched down!

Poor little snowflake,
With such a short life,
A dainty, pretty little thing,
Oh why, why did you have to die?

Sophie Glover (12)
Edgbaston High School

Handprints!

There used to be so many
Of my small handprints to see
On furniture and walls and things
From sticky, grubby me.

But if you stop and think awhile
You'll see I'm growing fast
Those little handprints disappear
You can't bring back the past

So here's a small reminder
To keep, not wipe away
Those tiny hands and how they looked
They'll make you smile someday!

Tiyana Athwal (12)
Edgbaston High School

Giant Blizzard

Giant blizzard run away,
As the icebergs shatter and break,
There's no time to sit around and play
Seeing that our lives are at stake!

Giant blizzard spare our lives,
Your draught is like 1000 knives,
I'm sick and tired of begging all the time,
Now I'm going to tell you what I don't like.

Giant blizzard in the middle of May!
We could live with you any day,
So go away or stay but if you choose to stay
You'll make the horses neigh!

Giant blizzards aren't so tough,
However the wind inside them is very rough!

Amandeep Bindra (12)
Edgbaston High School

I Wish I Was Tall

I wish I was tall!
Older girls towering over me
As if I'm a ball.

People think that I'm in Year 7!
Do they think that I'm eleven?

Girls rushing down the staircase for lunch,
They push me away and start to munch.

Why can't I be tall?
Let's face it . . . I'm nothing
                            but small!

Inderveer Dhanda (12)
Edgbaston High School

Beauty

Beauty has its charming ways
You could sit and look at it for days
Find a star! An 'angel face'!
I can't seem to find a trace.

If beauty comes with pain or sorrow,
I'm not willing to even follow,
The rules of being 'Your Majesty;
But oh, why can't that be me?

A shine, a glimmer of certainty,
Just to find some pure beauty,
But for now I'll just have to accept the fact,
There's none left and that is that!

So if you plan to find some charm,
Or walk down the red carpet arm in arm,
Or even up upon a shelf . . .
Sit down before you hurt yourself!

Samantha Cobb (12)
Edgbaston High School

Missing You

Oh how I miss you
No word can describe
And no sword can stop me.

I pray for you every night
With sorrow and delight.
Everything that you did for me
Made my life reasonable.

All those times we spent together
All those memories we made together
Flying by the angels' wings
Made a star each day.

Alice Lee (12)
Edgbaston High School

Is This Reality?

The world seems blurry,
through tired, confused eyes,
every day the same pain,
sometimes dreaming, sometimes living.
Why did the world change?
Pills and medicines instead of
laughter and fun,
as I sit in my wheelchair,
I am all alone.
The doctors say I'm mental,
that I see the world all wrong,
'You will never be cured,'
I hear them say,
'You can never be like anyone else.'
I disagree with them,
the world is exactly how I see it,
harsh, dangerous, cruel and depressing,
not beautiful or miraculous,
I hate the world, it can never be right for me,
my question is just this,
'Is this reality?'

Chloë Walford (12)
Edgbaston High School

Cousin

S hining, smiling and always sharing
C ute and cuddly like a bear
A ngelic like an angel, one who is never scared
R osy cheeks and bright red lips
L aughing all the time
E nergetic and exciting, all in one.
T his is my cousin . . .

                           Scarlet.

Kate Sparrow (12)
Edgbaston High School

Peace Or Pain

Pain is green and bumpy.
Pain tastes bitter and burnt.
Pain is a groaning, grinding, grating, to set your teeth on edge.
Pain smells rotten and damp.
Pain is dark corridors leading ever on, on.

Peace is white and fluffy.
Peace tastes pure and clean.
Peace is the calm and quiet of a gently running stream.
Peace smells fresh and new,
    - is a white dove skimming the clouds.

Envy is black and rough and hard,
Envy is completely tasteless.
Envy is the relentless screaming of a child who's lost their way.
Envy is a dark hole never ending, swallowing you up whole.
Envy smells of nothing, there is nothing to smell.
Envy is a dwindling light, growing fainter and fainter, until it has
    completely gone, never to re-light.

Joy is bright yellow, vibrant and strong.
Joy tastes fruity and sweet.
Joy is the laugh of excited children playing in the street.
Joy smells like sticky toffee pudding, smothered in chocolate sauce.
Joy is a smiley sun, shining down on this smiley world!

Anger is red and very hard and smooth.
Anger tastes salty like seawater.
Anger is a roaring wind, cutting at your face.
Anger smells of smoke and soot,
    and is watching the bus disappear around the corner!

Justice is gold, it sparkles in the sun.
Justice tastes smooth and creamy.
Justice is the song of a nightingale, sweet in the glowing sunrise.
Justice smells of a thousand poppies blowing in the wind.

Boredom is grey, grey as the world's *greyest* grey.
Boredom tastes dry and flavourless.
It is the slow persistent hum of a fly, flitting between the desks
    of sleeping children.
Boredom has a smell of petrol, very strong and acidic.
Boredom is your maths lesson - *zzzzz*.

Love is pink and red and green, orange and blue, too!
Love tastes sweet and sour sometimes.
Love is a party, a big noisy one, with heaps of balloons!
Love smells of champagne and lots and lots of chocolates.
Love is what holds this world together, stops it from falling apart!

Aimée Presswood (12)
Edgbaston High School

Green!

Green is a colour,
A colour that's cool.
All who despise it
Are considered a fool!

Grapes are quite tasty,
They are green too.
I'll take a grape
And give it to you.

Green is the fashion,
The fashion today.
Green is much better
Than pink, brown or grey!

Green is a colour,
A colour we love.
With vines of the ivy
And wings of a dove.

Green is the grass,
Green is *the* thing!
Green is the colour
Of your emerald ring.

No more ideas left,
Green's out of stock,
All I can say is
That green totally *rocks!*

Nadia Khan (12)
Edgbaston High School

If

(Based on Roald Dahl stories)

If George's grouchy granny can whizz up to the sky,
Then why does my granny stand
Only three feet high?

If Matilda can send homework away with her magic powers,
Why do I have to do it
With a pile of books as high as towers?

If Charlie Bucket owns a chocolate factory and eats as much

as he can,

Why do I have to eat fruit
Because chocolate has a ban?

If witches have the sources to turn boys into mice,
Why didn't they come a long time ago
And make the world a paradise?

If the Twits are so dirty and rude to each other,
Why am I in trouble,
With one rude word to my brother?

If James' giant peach can sail the ocean blue,
Then there can't be anything,
That I can't do!

Rachel Bleetman (12)
Edgbaston High School

Anger

It is as red as a volcano explosion
Anger sounds like a lot of fireworks banging in the sky
It tastes like red-hot chilli peppers
Anger smells like mouldy fish and fairy cakes
It looks like a red monster running after me
It reminds me of blood dribbling down my face.

Chloe Smith (11)
Edgbaston High School

Our House

Am I standing here on my own?
Why is this road too long to see?
Are those clumps of hay brushing by me?
Is this the feeling of cold autumn air?

Why suddenly did the air start to smoke?
Why did the flames get higher and higher?
Why are my eyes getting wider and wider?
Who is shouting and crying?
Was it me who started it?
Is this real
Or is it just a dream?

Natasha Joseph (12)
Edgbaston High School

The Mighty Reds

My team plays in red,
They knock the other teams dead,
They always beat the Blues,
And they never lose.

My favourite player is Steven Gerrard,
Because he is the best,
Scores better than the rest,
And would never dream of leaving my favourite team.

But when he is injured,
The game just isn't the same,
I much prefer it when he is playing,
That is why Liverpool's my team!

Steph Bostock (12)
Edgbaston High School

Life Of Riley, (The Cat)

What to do?
What to do next?
A stretch, a yawn,
Or maybe a nap?
I've made up my mind
I'll go for a stroll
Round to the neighbour's
To snooze on their bench
I wake, I scratch, a nice quick wash
My tummy rumbles, my mind's alert
I hop over the fence, I scratch at the door
A big bowl of food, what more could I want?
My belly full, now time for fuss
A lap to choose - a decision to be made
His looks good, but he's reading 'The Times'
Tough luck, mate, I'm coming up
A stroke to the head and a tickle under the chin
Ahh! The life of a cat - it's just *purrrfect!*

Holly Edwards (12)
Edgbaston High School

For You, Grandad

You brought warmth and brightness into my life,
that has now gone and all that is left is winter's coldness.

Every time you hugged me, you were a big bear
putting his arms around his baby cub.

You were my shining summer sunshine,
and that sunshine shall never fade.

Peacefully you went, but the love in my heart
for you shall never end.

Katie Moen (12)
Edgbaston High School

Animal Madness

(Nonsense poem)

There once was a big mouse,
That couldn't fit into his house
So he lay on a pie,
Until morning came by.

There once was a huge rat,
Who was bigger than a cat.
He ate a wasp for his tea,
For dessert, swallowed a bee.

There once was a baby zebra.
Who claimed that magic was *'abracadabra'*,
He told his mum he could turn his toy,
Into a very big, fat, ugly boy.

So the baby zebra,
Said, *'Abracadabra,'*
And, *bang!* The little toy
Became a very big, fat, ugly boy.

Merna Muharib (13)
Edgbaston High School

Happiness

Happiness is like friends
who play with you all day.

Happiness is like a family
that blow your worries away.

Happiness is a smile
that never goes away.

Happiness is love
that brings us all together.

Charlotte Payne (12)
Edgbaston High School

Rainbow

Red is like the colour of blood,
that pumps through our veins.
Orange is like the autumn leaves,
that fall from the trees.
Yellow is like a field of daffodils,
that stretch for miles and miles.
Green is like a juicy lime,
that tastes very bitter.
Blue is like the great, big, wide sky,
on a sunny day of the holidays.
Indigo is like a juicy plum,
that tastes sweet and sour.
Violet is like a violet flower,
with roots and leaves and a stalk.
Rainbow colours are like people,
they are everywhere!

Siân Morgan (11)
Edgbaston High School

My Neighbour

You don't want to meet my neighbour,
He is a very strange man.
His hair is like a nutty professor,
And his car is a 7-foot van.

My neighbour loves his garden,
As he's always peering over the wall.
He doesn't need a ladder,
Because he is very, very tall.

My mum and I went round to his,
To ask if he wanted some tea,
But he was in his underwear,
So we didn't want to see.

Olivia Maguire (12)
Edgbaston High School

Some Sisters . . .

Some sisters are boring,
Some sisters are fun,
Some sisters like drawing,
Some sisters laze in the sun.

Some sisters like shopping,
Some sisters like work,
Some sisters like hopping,
Some sisters go berserk.

But my sister is none of these things,
She has to be the best,
With sparkling earrings and necklaces,
She's better than all the rest.

Abbie Wright (14)
Edgbaston High School

My First Love

My first love was not a boy
Not greasy, fat and coy
But mine was soft and sweet
His tiny face so neat.

But alas my toy got thrown away
Down into the garbage chute to decay
The doctors said it would cause disease
'It makes you go weak at the knees.'

He was my very best friend
Who saw me to his very end
Whenever I needed someone there
He was always there to care.

Camilla Middleton (12)
Edgbaston High School

When I Win The Lottery

When I win the lottery
I'll have a load of money
instead of having jam on toast
I'll have caviar and honey.

When I win the lottery
I'll buy a new wardrobe
I'll get things from expensive shops
and from all around the globe.

When I win the lottery
I'll buy a house in Spain
I'll live a life of luxury
and I'll never work again

When I win the lottery
I'll buy a house of gold
I'll be covered in cosmetics
and I'll never look too old

When I win the lottery
I'll be a celebrity
I'll buy a place in Parliament
and everyone will follow *me*

But when I win the lottery
I'll still remain myself
having everything won't change me
even clothes and shoes and wealth.

Martha Davies (12)
Edgbaston High School

Shouts

Their shouts do not reach me,
Where I am,
I can hear them not.
I am no longer troubled by voices,
I cannot hear them.
A spectator of life,
I watch the world go by,
A spare part,
Ignored.

My parents are still weeping,
Crystal tears falling fast,
Seeming to never stop,
Grieving for a life broken,
But I'm not.
I still feel,
Anger, pain, sorrow, touch,
All emotions and senses I possess.
Missing only sound.

Their shouts do not reach me,
Where I am.
Hands do the talking now,
Signs replace words.
I can no longer hear them,
Their shouts cannot reach me.

Rebecca Tatlow (13)
Edgbaston High School

Space And Planets

Space is like a black sea with colourful planets.
Planets are like balls with bright, pretty patterns.
Pluto is like an ice cube, far away from the burning sun.
Neptune is like a ball of bubblegum ice cream.
Uranus is like a round, turquoise eyeball.
Saturn is like a person's finger with golden rings.
Jupiter is like an orange marble and a chimney
                                    always producing gas.
Mars is like a rock with a barren surface like the Wild West.
Earth is like a green and blue ball inhabited by humans.
Venus is like Venus Williams, it's very fast moving around the sun.
Mercury is like a hot fire jawbreaker because it is red
                                    and burning hot.
Space is like a sparkly blanket spreading over millions and
                                    millions of miles.

Pavithra Babu (11)
Edgbaston High School

Smiles

Smiles can be real
Smiles can be fake
Smiles can mean anything
Depends on your take!
A smile is better than wearing a frown
It hides all those things that are getting you down
Whoever you are
Whatever you do
Someone will smile
And you'll smile too!

Beki Hart (13)
Edgbaston High School

Snow

The snow is like cotton wool,
falling from the sky.

The snow is like a puffy cloud,
exploding into pieces.

The snow is like bite-sized sweets,
dropping onto the ground.

The snow is like buds,
falling from the trees.

The snow is like vanilla Maltesers,
building into a sweet snowman.

The snow is like white petals,
drifting in the sky.

Sukhmanie Sembhy (11)
Edgbaston High School

The Seaside

The beach is where I like to be,
Splashing, paddling in the sea.
Lots of children having fun,
Running around in the sun.
Relaxing, exciting, enjoyable too,
Throwing and catching is what kids like to do.

The giant waves crash on the shore,
All the surfers wanting more.
Frisbees, kites and balls in the air,
A grandma reading on a deckchair.
When I have had a lovely day,
I'm very sad to go away.

Rebecca Hicks (11)
Edgbaston High School

The Moon

The moon is like a piece of cheese
Which sometimes looks half-eaten.
The moon is like an owl
Which only comes out at night.
The moon is like a ship
Sailing in the deep blue.
The moon is like a unicorn
All mystical and gleaming.
The moon is like a dark room
Though reflected by the light.
The moon is like a family
Surrounded by the stars.
The moon is a strange thing
As last night it had disappeared!

Kate Finch (12)
Edgbaston High School

Animals

An elephant is like a loud drum,
Roaring and thumping.
A mouse is like a quiet countryside in winter,
Soft and still.
A gazelle is like an elegant pony,
Prancing along the long, green grass.
A rabbit is like a fluffy cotton bud,
Twitching and sniffing.
A fox is like a sly spy,
Prowling and barking.
And what am I like?
I'm like a cheeky acrobat,
A monkey!

Emma Kilby (11)
Edgbaston High School

Love

Love is such a happy thing,
Calling in the night.
Love is quite a sweet thing,
But love can be a fright.

Time spent is love,
Time to come is love.
Warm, cuddly and pink.
Scarlet, purple and blue is love,
Love makes you think.

Colours are love.
Scarlet and blue,
Orange and yellow,
Pink and red too.
Colours are love
And I love you.

Joanna Hughes (11)
Edgbaston High School

The Zoo

The snake is like a bar of soap
Sliding and slithering across the floor.
An elephant is like a big, loud drum
Thumping and banging, scaring everyone.
The tiger is like a gang of hunters
Waiting to catch their prey.
The penguins are like a line of dominoes
Being knocked down into the water.
Flamingos wandering in their pond
Like elegant ladies going to a dance.
The iguana in his tank
Lying still like a statue.

Alice Holtom (11)
Edgbaston High School

Anger

Anger
Is as red as boiling lava,
Hot and always bubbling.

Anger is a fierce, roaring lion
Forever ready to pounce.

Anger
Is emotional,
Sometimes mad, sometimes upset.

Anger
Is like a drum,
Annoying and always pounding.

Anger
Is a lemon,
Juicy and bitter.

Emma Noone (12)
Edgbaston High School

Love

I did not want to say goodbye this morning
as my father went to war,
I kept being told the bad things that would happen
by all my friends galore,
I would do anything for him to stay at home
and love me all the same,
I would run through a storm bare-footed
and cover myself in mud,
If he would just stay at home and continue
to give me his love.

Pollyanna Bell (12)
Edgbaston High School

The School Song

Teaching, and sometimes striving,
Wondering how best to get along
Practices, they cause confusion
And writing, the chatting's just far gone!

Teaching and sometimes striving,
Wondering how best to get along
Traipsing up to chemistry,
Phew! You got be strong!

Teaching and sometimes striving,
Wondering how best to get along
No homework today!
Thanks Mr Wong!

Teaching, no longer striving
Wondering how best to get along,
The last day of school today
So join in the school song!

Georgina May Kiely (12)
Edgbaston High School

Calmness

Calmness is violet like the petal of a bluebell,
Dancing softly in the breeze.
It sounds like a hymn being sung by two choirs.
It tastes like hot chocolate, keeping me warm inside.
It smells like different flowers, with different scents and all.
It looks like a floating bed, on a calm ocean.
It feels like kneading bread, letting out all my worries.
It reminds me of my best friend, Rachel, who tries to calm me down!

Alicia Cipolletta (11)
Edgbaston High School

The Mountain's Castle

Through the trees is a castle,
It overlooks the valley.
Bats and owls fly by.
The castle looks eerie.
What's inside?
Few know the truth.
Maybe there's a monster
Kids get dared to come in,
Never going back out.

There's no monster
I'm one of the few.
I know the truth.
I've been inside that castle
It's true.
I've never come out.
I'm not one of the kids
I'm the one.
The supposed monster,
But I wouldn't hurt a fly.
I'm merely a spirit wandering.

Sophie Brookes (13)
Edgbaston High School

Love

Love is pink like a beautiful rose.
Love sounds like a harp being sweetly played.
Love tastes like a box of Milk Tray chocolates.
It smells like exotic perfume.
Love looks like people cuddling.
It feels like a fluffy, soft cushion.
Love reminds me of a pink rose in a flower bed
Surrounded by beautiful flowers.

Sarah Howell (11)
Edgbaston High School

Just Behind The Door

I walked and walked
Day and night
Till I finally reached the door
I went in, it was dark and grim
And this is what I saw . . .

I saw a man with wrinkled hands
He gave me such a fright
He was old and grey
He turned away and vanished in the night.

Who was that man?
I wonder now,
Why did I dream his face?
Could it be he's showing me
That this was once his place?

Emily Greig (11)
Edgbaston High School

My Fears

The foggy colour of grey, all too similar to a dark mist,
Screams like dying children in the darkness of the night,
A taste of sour blood throughout the dryness of my mouth,
All remind me of my fears while in the dark, black night.
The smell of burning rubber,
And pictures of blood-sucking bats,
Plus the clamminess around me,
The tread of creaking floorboards while lying in my bed,
All haunt my waking dreams . . .

Robyn E Baxter (11)
Edgbaston High School

Stares

When I walk along the street,
Hordes of people pass me by,
They shoot me scornful looks,
That make me want to cry.

I know what they're gawping at,
I don't know why I should care.
But all my life I've lived with it,
I suppose they can't help but stare.

It spreads out over half my face,
Like ivy on an old stone wall.
It's big, burgundy and throbbing,
No one is ever nice, no one at all.

I've always had to live with it,
Throughout my life it's been always there,
Why was I born with this awful mark?
Why me? It really isn't fair.

Josie Smith (13)
Edgbaston High School

Laughter

Sky-blue laughter,
Like thousands of chattering people,
Tastes like a jar of candy.
Smells like the sweetest perfume,
Looks like cheeky monkeys,
Like me making faces behind
My brother's and sister's backs.
Feels like the happiest moment in life,
Reminds me of the funniest clown.

Renu Suthi (11)
Edgbaston High School

Squirrel

Like a bolt of lightning he darts up the gnarled oak tree
A mere blur of scarlet fur
Dominating the summer sunset with his vivid hue
So rare a colour we behold in this world of grey
Heart pounding he scarpers up the narrowest branches
Desperately clinging to peeling bark
Skilfully leaping from tree to tree - no obstacle can divert him
Tail rippling furiously, beating against the whipping wind
Icy rain cuts through his short bristled coat yet he never stops.
Suddenly he freezes in his tracks, quivering in fear
No predator he sees
Tentatively cocks one velvety ear, and listens to the world
Then with a bold jump, he skips lightly onto the ground below
To frolic amongst the spectrum of leaves
A glint of mischief sparkles in those beady eyes
Before dancing triumphantly back to the dray.

Janam Nagra (11)
Edgbaston High School

Love

Love can be peaceful
Although hearts can be broken
People can be happy
People can be sad
Romance is touching
Moving and special
Walks in the park
Holding hands, embracing
Love is fragile
Delicate as a flower
Wrap it up safely
And treasure it forever.

Rachel Learmonth (11)
Edgbaston High School

Infancy

Endless cries of
'What's the magic word?'
'Want a milk please'
Is all that is heard.

A laugh, a clap,
A pat on the head,
Just give her a Smartie
And send her to bed.

A flutter of lashes,
An angelic look,
A hopeful plea of
'Just one more book!'

A smile, a hug,
A kiss on the cheek,
Your heart melts like butter
As you sing her to sleep.

You come home from school,
Tons of homework to do,
You open the door
And it sounds like a zoo.

There she sits like the Queen Bee,
'How old are you Anna?'
The answer is . . . 'Three!'

Alice E Higgins (12)
Edgbaston High School

Love

Love is as red as a rose,
Love is like the sound of birds singing
Love tastes as sweet as sherbet
Love looks as heavenly as Heaven
Love feels as fluffy as a candyfloss cloud

Love reminds me of hearts red as blood.

Taymina Cabrita (11)
Edgbaston High School

The Second Person

'You are your generation,'
They used to say.
'You are the future,'
But who are they?

'You are your world.'
They used to say.
'You keep us healthy,'
But who are they?

'You are the Alpha and the Omega,'
They used to say.
'You'll breathe our last breath,'
But who are they?

'You are the hope for tomorrow,'
They used to say.
'You are the pinnacle of our achievements.'
But who were they?

Roshina Iqbal (13)
Edgbaston High School

The Wrinklies

Toothless and old, they look sincere,
'Pardon me, I didn't quite get that dear!'
They are all turning into wrinkly prunes,
All wrinkled up like a sea of sand dunes.
Their false teeth pop out,
Their hearing aids in.
They can't tell the difference between a TV and a bin,
They smell like a sea of flowery musk,
Their faces all white and their hair full with dust.
Their specs are as big as windowpanes
And made from the metal of World War II planes.
Although they are all dirty, old and grey,
They deserve the respect - they were us yesterday.

Hannah Cuthbert (11)
Edgbaston High School

The Bogeyman

My mommy said to me one day,
'You shouldn't pick your nose.'
She told me and she tells me,
'The bogeyman will know.'
I really didn't believe her,
Until one night in bed,
I was diving and delving in my nose,
And a deep voice said,
'The bogeyman will get you,
When you least expect.
The bogeyman will get you,
And you will certainly regret,
Picking and poking in your nose,
Or putting your hand near it.
Don't ever say you don't believe,
Cos the bogeyman will hear it.'
From that moment on,
I never did want
The bogeyman to visit.
And now I know,
Not to pick my nose
Cos the bogeyman will see it.

Alexandrea Kerr (14)
Edgbaston High School

My Sister

My little sister is very cute
Although we always get into disputes
She always gets me into trouble;
(This means that she bursts my bubble)!
Once she took my favourite rubber
When I found out I pushed her over
Even though we always fight
I still think that she's quite bright!

Daleep Sidhu (12)
Edgbaston High School

The Castle

The castle used to be filled with life, laughter and joy,
It was always busy and full of people, every girl and boy.
There were children running, chasing ducks and a hen,
There were blacksmiths, bakers and a goat, escaped from his pen.
There were jousting tournaments, held by the king,
And when it was over, everyone would dance and sing.

But now it is a ruin, desolate and bare,
It is on its own, no one goes there.
It is stood on a hill, eerie and dark,
You can hear nothing, not even a dog bark.
The castle wants to be lived in, it wants *happiness* to share.
But there is no happiness left.
There is nothing.

Francesca Wernham (11)
Edgbaston High School

Anger/Peace

Anger is . . . red!

An annoying sibling pestering you
A brother watching Power Rangers
Having to eat broccoli
Going on a boring fishing trip
Going to the dentist.

Peace is . . . turquoise

Relaxing knowing that you are safe in your bed
Rowing a boat across a calm lake
A comfortable armchair by the fire
Reading a good book to yourself quietly
Skating along my road.

Shirin Khanom
Edgbaston High School

Break Time

The doors open wide,
Children run out,
Freedom for ten minutes,
They can do what they like.

They shout and they cry,
They run and they play,
It's their time,
They can do what they like.

The playground fills up,
Full of laughter and fun,
Talking and chattering,
They can do what they like.

'Tig,' shouts a girl that's on,
'I'm stuck,' shouts another one that's caught,
'Bet you can't beat me,' says a girl that's just joined in,
They can do what they like.

The teacher comes out,
Everyone stops,
The bell rings . . .
Silence . . . !

Kate Nicholls (12)
Edgbaston High School

Teachers

T eachers can be strict, helpful and generous
E ach one possesses lots of different features
A teacher has to be intelligent for the job
C aring but can be strict if you can make them angry
H elpful if you lose something or if you're not feeling well
E very teacher teaches pupils different subjects
R eally talented, they must be to teach others
S ome are men, some are women but they're all unique
in their own special way.

Emily Price (11)
Edgbaston High School

The Little Match Girl

She stood on the pavement,
Her bony legs were white,
She shivered and her clothes were torn,
I felt the cold, I felt the pain in her heart,
She called out to folk along the street,
Her voice was faint,
They wouldn't buy from the little match girl,
They would only scrunch their faces in disgust,
A pearly tear rolled down her filthy black neck,
Her arms were bruised from her unsuitable bed,
The damp, cobbled street.
The girl collapsed and I caught her,
She was a feather,
I took her in,
She coughed up blood and I cried,
I cried for her,
She stumbled and scraped at the table of food with her fingernails,
And I fed her,
Although I provided her with a warm bed and healthy meal,
She still suffered and blood clung to her throat,
Again she collapsed and I caught her.
A doctor visited and his efforts were weak,
I stayed by her day and night,
Then one morning she did not awake
She had collapsed and I had not caught her!

Nikhila Patel (11)
Edgbaston High School

Love

Love is the colour of a red, velvet rose,
It sounds like a cat purring by a roaring hot fire,
It tastes like rich chocolate hearts with a creamy strawberry centre,
It smells like a candlelit dinner, ready for guests,
It looks like a steamy hot bath with red petals floating around,
Love reminds me of a shower of hearts!

Holly Ashworth (11)
Edgbaston High School

My Birthday List!

It's my birthday soon and I can't wait!
I'd better make a birthday list before it gets too late!
First I'd like a shiny, silver scooter,
But an electric one with a really loud hooter!
Next I'd love some glow in the dark stars,
And a spaceship that could fly me all the way to Mars!
I'd also adore a widescreen TV,
And to appear on the set of 'Casualty'!
Next up, there's a new pair of jeans,
And the world's largest trampolines!
You could provide me with some expensive jewellery,
But not the tacky stuff worn by Cat Deeley!
Lastly I want a brand new trombone,
And a really stylish mobile phone!
So you see, I'm not asking for much this year,
But you better get buying because my birthday is near!

Hannah Wishart (13)
Edgbaston High School

Anger

Anger is red like blood on my pillow after a nosebleed.
Anger sounds like my head after doing a headstand
                                    (oh my thumping head).
Anger tastes like horrible pheasant pate.
Anger smells like the exhaust fumes from my quad bike.
Anger looks like Brussels sprouts bubbling in the pan.
Anger feels like unsanded wood when I touch it.
Anger reminds me of raging boy racer cars.
Anger makes me want to stomp up and down on the stairs,
                                    so hard I could break them!

Amanda Huggins (11)
Edgbaston High School

Autumn

Autumn looks like a landscape of falling leaves.
Gold, brown, orange, red,
crispy yellow, auburn, clay.
Piling up high, high in the sky.

Autumn sounds like the wind howling
like a growling old granny!
And like the weeping of a nearly bare tree
that's lost all its money!

Autumn smells like chimney smoke
and a warm smoky fireside.
Oh no! All that smoke!
I think my lungs are going to explode!

Autumn tastes like caramel sweets
that stick to your gums
and never come off.
And like a hot cup of pumpkin juice
that scares you to bed!

Autumn feels like a gentle breeze
that makes you start to sneeze.
Autumn, autumn
You are a season of a kind.

Martha Gendy (12)
Edgbaston High School

Fear

Black as bats
Sounding of a scream
Tasting of blood
Smelling of sweat
Looking like a big, hairy spider
Feeling like a slippery grip
Reminding me of my sister in the morning.

Stephanie Bache (11)
Edgbaston High School

The World

The world is covered, a blanket of snow,
When people are celebrating, season of giving.
Trees are covered, the whole world is.
Whilst we are celebrating, animals are hibernating.

The world is covered in flowers sewn onto green patchwork,
When it is the time of birth.
Flowers open their little heads, the sun begins the day.
Trees are being decorated, beautifully shaped leaves.
The animals come out to play.

The world is brightening up, sun comes out to play.
The leaves begin to change, golden coloured crisps.
The sea is shimmering like sapphire, waving to the wind.
The sky is a blue blanket, decorated with fluffy cotton.

The world is at its colourful time.
Leaves turn into different colours, floating off like feathers.
The tree loses its decoration, prepares for the cold season.
Squirrels are climbing and running like insects,
Searching for their food.
Time is running out, they need to prepare,
It's a long sleep . . .

Queena Long (11)
Edgbaston High School

Love

Love is the colour of pretty pink tulips,
It sounds like beautiful soft music,
It tastes like strawberry creamy marshmallows,
It smells like melting chocolate in your mouth.
It looks like a butterfly fluttering by,
It feels as soft as a kitten's coat,
It reminds me of bursting hearts.

Catherine Thexton (11)
Edgbaston High School

Peace/Anger

Peace . . .
Is a gentle wave lapping on the shore,
Is a pure white cloud floating in the sky,
Is a shimmering, amber sunset,
Is a thick, purple mist on the horizon,
Is a golden beach with aqua-blue water,
Is a silver moonlight silhouetting the dark trees.

Anger . . .
Is as wild as a whirling tornado!
Is as hot as scorching flames!
Is as powerful as an erupting volcano!
Is as red as boiling larva!
Is like a blizzard holding you captive in the snow!

Sophie Barrett (12)
Edgbaston High School

Sadness

A flower standing by itself,
A park without any children,
A man without any friends,
It all stands for sadness.
Sadness can be shown in many ways,
Or not shown at all.

A raindrop is the tear of an angel,
A person without any family,
Or even a person without a smile,
Nobody knows how to stop it,
And do you know what?
That's the saddest thing of all!

Riti Dasgupta (11)
Edgbaston High School

My Poem About Music

Bartok, Brahms, Mozart and Clementi.
Beethoven, Sarasate, Chopin and Debussy.
The Carnival of the Animals, concertos,
Sonatas, 'The Planets', are all famous pieces.

Violin, viola, cello and bass,
Flute, clarinet, oboe and piccolo.
Trombone, trumpet and horn.
The banging of drums.
The crashing of cymbals.

There are some elements in music . . .
Dynamics, tone and pitch.
Keys, clefs, scores and staves.
Manuscript, timbre and texture.

There are different periods of time.
Bars and time signatures keep you in time.
Quartets, choir groups and trios.
Orchestras, courses and classes.

Exams, theory, aural and concerts
Auditions, rehearsals and musicals.

The woodwind section is made out of metal.
One kind of drum is called a kettle.
Rhythms are buzzing around
Making us tap our feet.
There is a silence, the orchestra stops.
It's the end of the piece.

Katherine Waller (11)
Edgbaston High School

Holidays Are In Three Minutes

Holidays are the best days,
Especially after school,
Waiting for the bell to ring
To run out and be cool.

Hours become minutes,
Minutes become seconds,
But there are still three minutes left,
Three more minutes, just three more minutes.

There are two minutes left,
Two more minutes.
We start to pack up frantically,
But our teacher just says, 'Calm down ladies,
We're not an elephant school!'

There's one more minute,
Just pass by soon,
We want to get out of here,
So we can shop like a loon.

Then the bell goes,
We all stand up and cheer,
Then we say to our teacher,
'See you next year!'

Now that school is over,
I'm going to make a rule,
To never ever in my life
Return back to school.

Jineesha Mehta (11)
Edgbaston High School

Anger . . .

Is like a red-hot chilli bursting onto other people
Is like a volcano erupting, burning, splashing everywhere
Is like a fire engulfing, scorching everything
Is like a huge, red monster eating away at friendships
Is like a roaring lion trying, trying to escape from a cage

Anger leads to danger
Anger leads to loss of control.

Victoria Nicholls (11)
Edgbaston High School

Peace

Peace is white as cream swirling in a jug.
Peace tastes like melted chocolate dribbling down my chin.
Peace is diving into a swimming pool on a hot summer's day.
Peace is hearing the ocean roaring at its best.
Peace looks like snow so still and soft.
Peace is having a red Ferrari and overtaking all those slow cars.
Peace feels like stroking soft puppies and having a great time.
Peace is when you're on cloud nine!

Rosanna Tomkins (11)
Edgbaston High School

Anger

Anger is a red-hot face,
With bursting veins.
Anger is a roaring fire,
Which causes pain.
Anger is a screaming sensation,
Hidden deep inside.
Anger is the dreadful emotions,
That we all want to hide.

Camilla Binns (11)
Edgbaston High School

Sweet Dreams

I dreamt last night
That all the world
Was made of sugar.
How sweet is that!

Trees were squashy sponge fingers.
The earth was wobbly jelly,
And the sea was made of creamy custard.
A *trifle* strange!

A colossal Double Decker
Carried stretchy liquorice people,
Like lots of Bertie Bassets.
It takes allsorts!

Sculptors moulded fudge into fabulous figurines,
While painters sketched on sugar paper
With their luscious fruit pastels.
Quite crafty!

Pearly white glacé icing snow
Dribbled over crunchy gingerbread mansions,
And candyfloss puffed from pink wafer chimneys.
Quality Streets!

The orchards were full of angelica trees,
Dripping with apple and pear drops,
Infested with wriggling chocolate worms.
Picnic time!

And far away, across the galaxy,
Whizzed millions of sherbet flying saucers,
And multicoloured ice-lolly rockets lit up the Milky Way.
They were all Space Invaders!

I woke this morning,
To find all the world
Was not made of sugar,
But life remained sweet all the same!

Sarah Baker (13)
Edgbaston High School

The Dead

The tombstone lay undisturbed for years,
Nobody visited it, nobody cared.
The corpse was withered and weak,
A bony hand lay outstretched next to the body,
In it, was a shiny bloodstained dagger.
It was old, yet looked recently used.
In fact it was recently used, on the dead body.
The soul was sucked out, and the spirit was destroyed,
The sniper of the dead was out to kill.
Not kill the humans, but to kill the afterlife.
The heart was removed from the body, and was crushed and burnt.
Some say it was a vandal,
Some say it went to Heaven.
But only I will ever know that it was, in fact, none of the reasons
people thought.

But a ghost, a devious demented ghost
Who was out to kill the souls of the dead.

Hannah Davis (13)
Edgbaston High School

Anger

Anger is the colour red,
Like a baby screaming
And an elephant stomping around.

Anger is being disturbed
And being beaten in a race by a cheetah.

Anger is missing the bus
And my friend going without me.

Anger is not getting my own way
And getting punched in the face by a human.

Helen Roberts
Edgbaston High School

The Game

Mesmerising children, from young to old,
Distracting them from what they've been told.
Confusing their minds with cartoons and controls,
Where Rayman punches hard and Lara Croft sneakily rolls.
When someone horribly tries to kill Harry Potter,
Well, showing little kids this is a different matter!

Where they look all day at a TV screen,
While handling controls with weird machines
Where they're addicted to the game, and you can't get them away,
And when they *do* speak, the only words you hear are,
'What did you say?'
They concentrate on the game so much, that they can't even hear
Them getting squared eyes is what I fear!

With violent kicks and shooting guns.
Is this what will happen when the future comes?

Laura Chung (13)
Edgbaston High School

Anger

Anger is an annoying sister,
It's red and burning with fury,
Anger is envy and jealousy
And is like a blister!

Anger is like a wild fire,
Like a snake's bite,
Anger is an exploding potion
And is what a lion desires!

Anger is like a storm stirring the sea up
And is like a wild tornado in a teacup!

Claudia Noon
Edgbaston High School

My Ideal Career

I don't want to work 'til seventy-five, then stop work,
Become immobile and then - well die!
I want to discover the world and all its truths,
Make a difference - maybe follow clues.
To fly a million miles above the Earth;
Not sit in an office doing work!
I want to see through another person's eyes
And then chocolate tasting I might try.
Or be a professional ballet dancer
- Or meet Santa and Rudolph, Dasher and Prancer!
I don't want a computer to take over my life;
To sit in front of a screen full of strife.
I could explore the seas and wrestle a lion,
Sail the seven seas, or build a bridge of iron.
Perhaps I could be an amazing Red Arrow,
Or trundle round town, selling veg in a barrow.
I would like this to be a world of mine;
No more paperwork - just plenty of time.
In it I could be a film director,
Or join the FBI - be head of my sector.
I want to do a job that will give something back;
Help someone someway - give something they lack.
I think I will be an entrepreneur;
Do a bit of everything - and give the world a stir!

Jennifer Mayhew (13)
Edgbaston High School

Anger

Anger is red blood rushing through my body.
Anger is a chilli burning my mouth.
Anger is the bus going straight past me.
Anger is being woken up on a Saturday.
Anger is fierce flickering flames trying to escape.

Harriet Bates (11)
Edgbaston High School

Hallowe'en

Hallowe'en is the best!
Better than all the rest

Jumping, screaming, going wild,
Scaring every little child

Trick or treating,
Hiding and seeking

Tonight's the night
You'll get a fright

Witches soaring
Vampires gnawing

Wolf men growling
Ghosts howling

Tonight's the night
You're going to scream

Because after all it's
Hallowe'en!

Hayleigh Pither (13)
Edgbaston High School

Peace Is . . .

Peace is white like light, white snow,
Peace sounds like a quiet spring morning in the countryside,
Peace tastes warm and sweet like chocolate melting in your mouth,
Peace feels calm and tranquil,
Peace is relaxing,
Peace is quiet,
Peace is Heaven.

Liberty Peters (12)
Edgbaston High School

Peace

As heavenly as a creamy pot of Philadelphia.
Sitting on a white, fluffy, dreamy cloud I could almost fall asleep on.
A Swiss chocolate slab, a whole bar of course!
A pale blue sky.
I'm on cloud nine.
Lovely and quiet, so dreamy.
In my room, the light turned dim.
In the edge of the room I snuggle in with a book,
As serene as it could be.
I step in my bed as warm as a heater,
With a cosy little duvet.
I imagine . . .

Simran Sidhu (11)
Edgbaston High School

Peace

Peace is blue-green like the calming ocean.
It is also like a bunch of pretty flowers.
Peace is a comfy bed.
It is also as quiet as a mouse.
Peace is as soft as a feather.
It is also being joyful.
Peace is as kind as your very best friend.
It is like a cute little kitten.
Peace is relaxing on a soft, sandy beach.

Nisha Jaswal (11)
Edgbaston High School

Once Again

The world just passes by,
And you're sat wondering why
Why did it happen to you?
Your first chance at something new
And as soon as you get close to it
It's snatched away bit by bit.

You'll sit alone,
Reducing to skin and bone.
Life just isn't the same,
It all changed the day he came.
His absence has led to your defeat.

It was the day he proposed
That it all went wrong.
You were just getting composed,
When you heard the gun,
That was the moment that you went numb.

A young, enraptured girl,
Sits in her derelict mansion,
Deprived of her passion,
Because he'll never come.

Looking at the trigger of the gun
It's started to look like the only way
She holds it to her head to be with her love,
Once again.

Sarah Learmonth (14)
Edgbaston High School

A Fire

Bang! Snap! Like a whip it cracks!
Fizz! Pop! Like a rabbit it hops!
Crackle! Whizz! Like cats that hiss!
Spit! Splutter! Like an endless mutter.

A bright light in the distance,
Or could it be panic or terror?
A red flower with smoke,
Or a ghastly thing of destruction?

A moonless, starless night,
Nothing, but darkness and flame,
And a gale of wind comes,
Unleashing its torrential rage!

Liana Easterby (11)
Edgbaston High School

My Family

My family:
    There's my mum,
She does everything.

    My dad,
He's a games master as well as a really good dad.

    My twin, David,
His pinches are fatal, they rip off the skin.

    My older brother, James,
He's alright except when we get into a fight.

    And then there's me,
Well, I'll let you decide about that!

Charlotte Mason (11)
Edgbaston High School

Animals

Scampering in-between people's feet,
Watching those thick rubber soles
That may one day
Bring about their death.

Eating cheese
Where they can
Watching out for traps
Snap, snap, snap!

Splashing through the waves
Jumping in and out
Squeaking cheerfully
Intelligent creatures they are

The two animals
Different but the same
Hoping to be understood
In the world.

Ellen Ewer (12)
Edgbaston High School

My Holiday

M y holidays are my favourite part of the year.
Y our holidays may be good but not as good as mine.

H olidays, holidays, holidays, always sunny and fun.
O range suns are always invited.
L ast year it was Paris, this year it's Cornwall.
I n France last year we tried to speak French (not very well).
D ifferent every year (hopefully).
A t least we try to be different anyway.
Y es! They are different, they get better every year.

Katie Johnston (11)
Edgbaston High School

A Ballet Performance

Standing in the wings
The curtain's down
The audience is listening
To the orchestra's sound.

Warming up my feet,
Point, point, point
Bending and stretching
Loosening my joints

The curtain rises
The audience is clapping
The sound dies away
And they all sit observing.

The principle dancers start,
Arabesques, pirouettes and leaps!
While everyone else waits in the wings
Occasionally having a peep.

Now it's my turn
I just simply can't wait!
I'm ready to go
But all my legs do is shake!

I take one big leap
Right across the stage
It feels *great!*
The audience just gaze.

The performance has been a hit
Everyone returns home smiling
Tomorrow I'll be back
With the silver lining!

Hannah Millward (11)
Edgbaston High School

Ice Skating

I ce skaters leap and glide,
C hilly hands, amazing mind,
E nchantment all around.

S mooth white ice,
K icks, flicks and swirls.
A s boots scrape across the ice,
T racks are carved in deep,
I ntuition takes over, off I go,
N othing can stop me now!
G liding across a frozen lake, I'm free!

Charlotte Towers (12)
Edgbaston High School

Winter Worlds

The whistling world torments the trees
and the ground is covered with crunchy leaves.
Winter's icy fingers grasp the world
and the people's toes are curled.

At night the angels come spreading a white carpet of snow,
Father Christmas flies over our rooftops, 'Ho, ho, ho!'

The east wind blasts away the warm air,
Robins shelter in the shrubs with furled wings
And as the snow flutters down it sweetly sings.

Tiny field mice silent scuttle to their fur-lined nest,
Hedgehogs hibernate and squirrels rest.

Melanie Jane Whitfield (12)
Edgbaston High School

Fairy-Tale Land

If you close your eyes
and imagine that you're in a fairy-tale land
Can you see the bed of chrysanthemums
the 14-coloured rainbow
over the dreamy colourless sky?

What can you see in your fairy-tale land?
Can you see the muffin man
Dancing in the wicked witch's sweet house
When you follow the route of Hanzel and Gretel's paths?

Fairy-tale Land is for you to imagine
What can you see?
What can you do
In your own fairy-tale land?

Yuki Ando (12)
Edgbaston High School

Winter

The winter days draw near,
Light turned to black coal,
Everywhere is deserted,
Like the world had lost its soul!

The people in the towns,
Waking up to something white,
Something wet and cold,
Something pale and something bright!

Christmas is on its way,
People doing the shopping in town,
Hanging up decorations,
Feeling excited deep, deep down!

Lizzie Paul (12)
Edgbaston High School

King Of The Night

When the sun turns to rest,
And the sky turns black,
The stars are diamonds,
Sprinkled like sugar over a deep blue, velvet cloth.

The owls start hooting,
And signal to their master,
For it is his turn to reign,
As king of the night.

He emerges from a misty, grey curtain of clouds,
He looks at his kingdom,
He is a silver medallion,
He is king of the night.

Luminous in the darkness,
He alone radiates,
A metallic shine of blinding beams,
King of the night.

A torch to the sunless sky,
Leading his people far away in sleep,
To dream and be free,
King of the night.

A king and his court,
The moon and his stars,
A candle and its glow,
The moon and its gleam.

The clouds are its crown,
The silent creatures, its people,
The hours of darkness, its kingdom,
King of the night.

Sabah Yaqoob (12)
Edgbaston High School

The Ocean

The ocean is like a big playground
for underwater creatures.
The ocean is like an underwater mystical land
where mermaids come out to play.
The ocean is like a never-ending book
because you never know what's going to happen.
The ocean is like a bubble machine
where bubbles never stop floating around.
The ocean is like a rainbow
because there are so many colours.
The ocean is like the sky
always changing colours.

Lydia John (12)
Edgbaston High School

The Spirit Of The Unicorn

As the moon shines with all her might,
Spreading her beam across the darkening night.
The fairies sprinkle their stardust around,
Flowers appear as each particle touches the ground.
Then appears a silvery horn,
This is the spirit of the unicorn.

This magic horse will stand where the stream,
Has a silvery look from the moon's strong beam.
With a coat as pure as snow,
That shimmers and sparkles amongst the glow.
And there it shall stand until the dawn,
This is the spirit of the unicorn.

Amy Hetherington (11)
Edgbaston High School

Christmas

Christmas is here and snowflakes are falling,
Swirling and whirling in the bright sky.
Upstairs in bed our parents are snoring,
Santa has taken the milk and mince pie.
Our Christmas tree stands tall in the morning,
Around it and under are presents piled high.

Finally our parents slump downstairs,
'Yippee!' we shout, jumping up and down.
Ripping open presents in our chairs,
Playing with our toys in our night-gowns.
Paper everywhere, who really cares?
There's so much happiness all around.

Emily Lane (11)
Edgbaston High School

A Friend

A friend is like a bath,
Warm and comforting.
A friend is like a present,
Full of surprises.
A friend is like a member of my family,
Who I can count on and trust.
A friend is like a pet,
Someone loyal and kind.
A friend is like my mum,
Helpful and nice.
A friend is like a never-ending bar of chocolate,
Bringing me happiness and joy.

Eleanor Davis (11)
Edgbaston High School

The Weather

The sun is like a ball of fire,
Turning the sky to ash.
The rain is like a baby crying,
In wait for some food to eat.
Thunder is like a great hall of people,
Clapping a successful show.
Lightning is like a lamp or light,
Being turned on and off.
The snow is like a plain white blanket,
Hail is like huge silver pennies,
Pouring down onto the earth.
A rainbow is like a painter,
Merging all colours together.
The weather is like a circle of friends,
Always changing to something different.

Natasha Perera (12)
Edgbaston High School

Smiles

S miles are really clever,
M any last forever and ever.
I love smiles, they're full of glee,
L ike buttercups, I can see.
E very smile makes me glad,
S miles are like big hugs from Dad!

S mile, smile, it makes you feel good,
M y heart is like a silver bud.
I 'm always happy, can't you see?
L ovely smiles belong to me.
E very smile can be free,
S mile and sing, you'll soon see!

Jenny Abrams (11)
Edgbaston High School

A Strawberry Tale

The round sweet strawberry growing in the field,
turning red and juicy,
with its leaves as its shield
from the bright red sunshine
high up in the sky,
allows my yummy strawberry
to ripen for a pie.

But sometimes when the sun don't shine
and the strawberries won't grow,
the farmer gets a glass of wine
because he's nowt to show.
No matter how much time he's given
the poor little strawberry won't keep livin'.

Jessica Hodson-Walker (11)
Edgbaston High School

Jobs

There was once a girl named Taylor
who did not want to be a sailor
she wanted to be a teacher
but everybody thought that she was a mean creature
until one day she became a teacher in religion
her lessons were fun because she was a magician.

Then she decided to be a firewoman
she was very good, she even saved a boy called Dan
she did not like that job so she became a dancer
everyone called her Dancer Prancer.
In the end that girl named Taylor
became a sailor.

Taylor Smietanski (11)
Edgbaston High School

Anger

Anger, red like warm dripping blood.
Sounds like a drum beating inside my heart.
Tastes like red-hot chillies.
Smells like burning wood.
Anger looks like the Devil himself.
It feels like a great ball of fire.
Reminds me of an erupting volcano.

Emily Moyce (11)
Edgbaston High School

Death

Death is both good and bad,
But when people suffer we always get mad,
But they're no longer in pain,
Even though we know that we will never see them again.

No matter how much we moan and cry,
We must all accept everyone must die,
The thought of it, to some, is frightening,
But to others when we die, life is just starting.

I think of death as a tree,
That just stands there peacefully,
I also think of death as a rose,
But a rose must wilt and we must die I suppose.

So don't be scared of dying,
Think of it as good,
Even though I know it's frightening,
Imagine you're going to see God in his garden and his wood.

When you get to those pearly gates,
Just remember, in this place there is no hate,
This place is peaceful and full of love,
Just like the flight of the beautiful white dove.

Aimee Crickmore
Four Dwellings School

1914

1914 is the year of Hell,
Because I knew I had to go.
Even though I didn't want to,
I knew I had to go.

After being enlisted and checked,
Off we went to Germany.
Marching away in front of you,
As we go and fight for you.

In the trenches high and wide,
We wait nervously with some pride,
We know we have to go soon,
But I would go any time now.

When that whistle blew,
That's when I knew,
That my life was on the line,
With others from trench nine.

Going over the top felt like an eternity,
But it seemed very right.
Guns blasting off,
Leaving devastation in its wake.

Going over the top did seem right,
But then I felt it,
A German's rage,
A bullet from a gun,
And then I knew,
That 1914 was the year of Hell.

Lee Savery
Four Dwellings School

Family Time

It's not the first droplet of snow
Or the last snowflake to fall
It's not the first snowball thrown
Or the last angel in the snow made

It's not the first present given
Or the last dinner eaten
It's not the first tree put up
Or the last lights taken down

It's not the first present wrapped
Or the last star wished on
It's not the first turkey carved
Or the last song sung

It's not the first to say, 'Merry Christmas'
Or the last to watch the play
It's not the first to dream of Santa Claus
Or the last to say goodnight

It's not the first to start the shopping
Or the last to build a snowman
It's not the first to open an advent calendar
Or the last to sing a carol
That makes Christmas special
It's family time.

Rebecca Tombs (13)
Four Dwellings School

Footsteps In The Snow

Footsteps in the snow
Cracks in the ice
Breath in the fog
Hail through the night

A child wide awake
A baby in its cot
A mother in her bed
A father out at work

Everyone freezing
Like ice cream in a fridge
The teachers in the staffroom
All snug and warm

A badger in its hole
A bird in its nest
A bee in its beehive
A shark in the sea

A winter comes to an end
A light shines through
Everyone is happy except me and you.

Gemma Tombs (11)
Four Dwellings School

I Love You

My heart is yours,
I can stay true,
You are so beautiful,
That's why I love you.

I need you always,
In my life,
Your face just looks,
So sweet and nice.

Please stay with me,
For evermore,
And behind us,
We can close the door.

Just us two here,
Just me and you,
So I will tell you,
That I love you!

Stuart Choudhury (13)
Four Dwellings School

Casper The Ghost

Casper is the name of a ghost
He is more smart and more friendly than most
He is fun, he is witty and he likes to play games
He likes all my friends and never calls names
He is always around for whenever I'm down
He cheers me up and acts like a clown
Casper I love you, now and always
My best friend you are and I hope you stay.

Kirstie Harrison (12)
Hillcrest School & Sixth Form

Typical Teenage Morning

You wake up in the morning
half an hour late
and think to yourself
my God what a state

Last night's mascara
smudges down your face
think to yourself
what a disgrace!

Then there's the hair
where on earth is the brush?
Oh you haven't got time
you're in such a rush

Up it goes
in that scruffy bun
I'm telling you now
this certainly ain't fun!

'Come on!' yells Mum
'You'll be late for school.
Flipping heck
you don't half look a fool

Well I suppose it's a start
you're out of bed
but with breath like that
you'll wake the dead.'

You make it to school
not paying attention
and you get yourself
a week of detention!

Victoria Ezugha (15)
Hillcrest School & Sixth Form

Animals In The Zoo

I'm yellow with black spots
Higher than the treetops
I eat leaves off the trees
But I don't attract fleas
Who am I?
Next question.

I swing about
I scream and shout
Bananas I eat
Touch my head with my feet
Who am I?
Next question.

I am black and white
Have millions of stripes
I am known on the road
Which I have been told
Who am I?
Next question.

I'm really, really fat
My ears flap and flap
I never ever forget
If I squirt you'll get wet
Who am I?

Jade Simms-Smith (13)
Hillcrest School & Sixth Form

Friends

Friends will come,
and friends will go,
the seasons change,
and it will snow.
But you are always in my heart
and we will never be apart.

Jodie Carter (14)
Hillcrest School & Sixth Form

The White Witch

The white witch,
queen of Cair Paravel.
A face cold and stark,
her lips were as red as
a furious beast's heart pumping blood!

With hands long and cold,
they shot out icy cold
snowballs!

When you looked into her eyes
you could see fire
'No'
actually they *were* fire!

If you had touched the queen you would instantly be
turned into rock-hard stone!
With death roaming upon you
all you could think of is *nothing!*

When she spoke you would feel an icy cold and stern voice
invading your earlobes!
It stays there torturing you for the rest of your living days!

When you stood near her, you couldn't move, it felt like a herd
of lions and cheetahs forming a circle around you!
Coming closer and closer!
All you could do is stand there watching and waiting!

Kirandeep Chumber (11)
Hillcrest School & Sixth Form

Winter

The cold breeze of the wind
The night's sky is early
Christmas cards and wrapping paper all in the shop windows
The crunching of the frost on the ground
Then the snow comes
Now it's really *winter*.

Laura Ling (13)
Hillcrest School & Sixth Form

My Difficult Day

Some shoes
a cruise

Difficult dilemma
cream cake or paella

My favourite jeans
that are sewn by the seams

My friends think they're funny
when they're spending my money

When I finish school
I go out to look cool

Then at 11, burst my bubble
as I switch off my favourite TV channel, Trouble

I hop into bed
and dream of boys that aren't named Fred

Oh my bedroom is a mess
goodnight and God bless.

Louise Fullerton (13)
Hillcrest School & Sixth Form

Beautiful

Every time I look into your face,
your loveliness I see,
even though you might not understand,
you are beautiful to me.

And sometimes you just can't see it
'cause it simply can't be seen,
because it's hidden in the quietness
like a gentle flowing stream.

Keena Laing (11)
Hillcrest School & Sixth Form

A Butterfly

A butterfly
that eats pollen and nectar,
a wise creature that sometimes
you can see in your garden,
going to different flowers.

There are many different colours
of butterflies,
some are colourful,
some are dull.

It flies slowly
and when it goes to the leaf,
it will lay its eggs
to be a caterpillar first,
but when it grows older
it will be a beautiful
and colourful butterfly.

Eisa Vanessa Velicaria (11)
Hillcrest School & Sixth Form

The Friendship Fairy

Radiant friend guiding me along.
By my side, forever strong.
As I sit and think of you
My heart is in tune because of you.
For every day you do not wane
Beside me is your place of gain.
For the love I give to you
Feed your heart as like me.
We share to gain love and comfort forever strong.
Oh thank you my guiding star, so bright, forever strong . . .

Ruby Mills (11)
Hillcrest School & Sixth Form

Tiger

The tiger, orange and black,
Black stripes, humped back,
Claws as sharp as string on a harp.

Teeth are pointed,
Paws are hoisted,
Eyes glare while they stare.

Are you there? Yes.
It's giving you a stare.
Wait, it's gone. Where is it?
Oh no, it's on you!

It's dangerous,
You can't move,
He bares his teeth,
You can't handle this.

You're struggling to move,
Distraction.
The tiger turns, runs,
You're safe.

Francesca Haines (11)
Hillcrest School & Sixth Form

Ice Cream

Ice cream! Ice cream!
You're wonderful stuff,
I love you, ice cream,
I just can't get enough.
You're covered with
All kinds of flavours,
And you're sprinkled with ice!
Ice cream! Ice cream!
Oh! Give me some please!

Seo Jung Lee (12)
Hillcrest School & Sixth Form

The Deep Blue Sea

The crashing against the rocks,
And the lovely cream white froth,
Upon the seabed the seaweed lies,
In the deep blue sea.

I can hear the sea,
I can see the surfers,
I can play,
In the deep blue sea.

I can feel the sand,
I can feel the sea,
I can play in the sand,
And I can play in the sea.

Lucy Whiston (13)
Hillcrest School & Sixth Form

Me

I'm all alone
No one's here but me
I'm all alone
No one can see me
But me
I'm far away
All alone
No one to see me but me
I don't understand why
Why I'm all alone
Looking at my reflection
No one can hear or see me
Except someone looking back at me
And that is me.

Siobhan Thompson (13)
Hillcrest School & Sixth Form

My Poem

When my teacher told me to write a poem
I didn't know what to write
A short one?
A long one?
One that rhymes?
One with atmosphere?
One with pictures?
One that is a riddle?
One with emotion?
One with passion?
One that is funny?
When my teacher told me to write a poem
I didn't know what to write

So I wrote a new kind of poem . . .
My poem.

Katie Ward (13)
Hillcrest School & Sixth Form

Hallowe'en

It's Hallowe'en, a time for fun,
The scary times have just begun,
All the young kids trying to look scary,
Some little girls dress as a fairy.

Witches and ghosts roaming the streets,
Scavaging for chocolate, money and treats,
Pumpkins and decorations are all around,
Knocking on doors for a penny or a pound.

Hallowe'en is the best celebration,
Celebrated all over the nation.

Jade McCalla (13)
Hillcrest School & Sixth Form

Children In Need

We need to help each other,
Mother, Father, Son, Brother.
Look at the bad world today,
People fighting for lives as they pray.

Look how fortunate we are,
Going to school and going far.
People needing, need a chance,
To see how far they'll enhance.

No one cares this day,
They work and don't get pay.
Just put your hand in,
All this trouble won't go in the bin.

In a few centuries they think,
Man will be extinct.
Because of all of you,
Just stand in the heavenly queue.

Rhia Walker (13)
Hillcrest School & Sixth Form

Autumn Poem

Now it's autumn
the leaves are falling!

Now it's autumn
the birds are calling!

Now it's autumn
the clouds are black!

Now it's autumn
the shadows are behind your back!

Elinor Davies (13)
Hillcrest School & Sixth Form

War

War is crazy,
War is mad,
War is always worse than bad.

War is poverty,
War is a curse,
War is always worse than worse.

War is crazy,
War is mad,
War is always worse than sad.

Countries lying,
Children dying,
Babies crying,
War!

Sarah Plant (12)
Hillcrest School & Sixth Form

The Sky

The sky, the sky
How I want to fly
Up to the sky.

To be up there
I would say a prayer
To bounce on the
Fluffy clouds.

It's blue like the sea
And it would clearly be
My one place in the world!

Sarah Steele (13)
Hillcrest School & Sixth Form

Curly, Curly Custard

Curly, curly custard
Green snot pie
All mixed together
With a dead dog's eye

What shall I put now?
Everyone's chin
Only now it's getting
A bit too thin.

Something for the flavour
Baby's sick
All mixed together
To make it really thick!

Lovelle Edmead (12)
Hillcrest School & Sixth Form

When The Ocean Is Sleeping

When the ocean is sleeping
It is peaceful and calm
When the sun rises
It awakes the ocean too
What a beautiful shade of blue

During the day when it likes to mess about
Clashing against the rocks is what it does best
The wind and the ocean
Are good friends you know
That makes so much noise you wouldn't know what to do
The ocean gets tired again, and starts sleeping away
What a beautiful shade of blue.

Simone Hyde (13)
Hillcrest School & Sixth Form

Hope

Hope keeps you going,
When you've been knocked down,
Hope makes you smile,
When you've a nasty frown,
Hope picks up the pieces,
And makes your problems go away,
It makes you ready for them,
If they come back another day,
So fear not, you are never alone,
As hope is always there,
It guides and it helps,
It's with you everywhere,
Sometimes it's hidden,
Deep in your heart,
And all you have to do is find it,
And you'll never be apart,
Because hope keeps you going,
When you've been knocked down,
And hope makes you smile,
When you've a nasty frown!

Zarah Taj (14)
Hillcrest School & Sixth Form

The 3Cs

Chocolate, chips and crisps,
That is all I need,
Forget the boring fruit,
Like apples, oranges and bananas,
They only taste good as a drink,
Sugar, fat and grease,
Mmmm, that is nice,
I'll eat it all my life.
Uh-oh, I'm obese.

Amrita Gill (12)
Hillcrest School & Sixth Form

Chocolate

Chocolate, chocolate
You're naughty stuff
I adore you so
I can't get enough
You're so devouring
Yet you add a few inches onto my waist
Chocolate, oh chocolate
Don't do this to me

So creamy, so indulging
Chocolate cakes, chocolate ice cream
Chocolate milkshake
And even chocolate mousse

Chocolate with caramel, chocolate with mint
Chocolate with orange, I love you all
Milk chocolate, white chocolate
And even dark chocolate
Chocolate, chocolate, I love you so
Chocolate, chocolate, I beg you so
Don't do this to me.

Naa Akle Dromo Okantey (12)
Hillcrest School & Sixth Form

Racism!

Black and white
Should do alright,
But!
Because they're white
Think they have the right,
But racism is really bad,
And can also be very sad,
But when you bully please remember
There is no black or white to fight!

Zoe McCusker (13)
Hillcrest School & Sixth Form

What A Bad Day

Waking up ready to start the day
thinking everything's gonna be OK.
First of all your hair won't go right
then your bobble's way too tight.
Your coffee goes nasty and cold
your bread and milk start to grow mould!
You get a breakfast takeaway
everything's going just your way.
You walk over to a bin
and trip over a rusty tin.
It has been a bad day
let's hope tomorrow will be OK!

Kirsty Hornsby (12)
Hillcrest School & Sixth Form

What Is It?

Quick runner
Loud roarer
Sharp claws
Filthy paws
Flesh eater
Animal beater
Hunter hider
Meat finder
Furry face
Always on the chase
His name is Brian
It's a . . .

Amana Youngsam (12)
Hillcrest School & Sixth Form

High In The Sky And Over The Sea

Oh how I would love to walk by the seashore
to get away from the living bore.

And open my wings and spread them wide
to see spectacular views once admired.

Fly high in the sky and through the clouds
up and down, so happy I am I screamed aloud!

Hover over hot pools, rocks and stones
bright colours of the creatures in the sea are shown.

Deep down under plants and mountains
volcanoes at sea shoot out lava fountains.

Treasure so strong and unique
creatures born every week.

High in the sky and over the sea
with a spectacular view in front of me.

Asaybi Snape (13)
Hillcrest School & Sixth Form

Pancakes

Into the pan the pancakes go
Don't forget a little oil though!

Flip them and toss them a lot
But watch they don't fall out, they're very hot!

On the plate they smell delicious
But don't touch them yet, the burns could be vicious!

A drizzle of syrup and a few chocolate chips
But don't eat too many, they go straight on your hips!

Hayley Breecher (12)
Hillcrest School & Sixth Form

Christmas Day

Christmas morning
I am yawning
Presents to open
Friends to phone
Everyone laughing
Everyone smiling

Christmas evening
Turkey roasting
Cousin groaning
Parents moaning
Quick, tidy up, family's here!
Dinner's gone
Family's gone.

Kelly Fletcher (12)
Hillcrest School & Sixth Form

Dogs!

Wake up in the morning,
Have a little stretch,
Come and have some dinner now!
Fetch, fetch, fetch!

Run around the garden,
Have a little rest,
Greet all the friendly people,
Come on, you're the best!

Go and hunt the bone down,
Curl up in a ball,
Now the little puppy dog,
Is making no noise at all.

Cassandra Nelson (12)
Hillcrest School & Sixth Form

My Friends

My friends always care,
And no matter what they're there,
As a shoulder to cry on they're great,
I really have the greatest mates.

They listen all the time,
They never act or mime,
When they talk they never cause a din,
And if there was a competition for best friends they'd definitely win.

We are all best mates - 24/7,
And my friends will definitely go to Heaven,
Because when I'm up or down,
They'll always be around.

So thank you my best mates,
For helping me with all those dates,
I will always be there for you,
And we will be friends forever, I know that's true.

Adele Gavin (12)
Hillcrest School & Sixth Form

After-School Remedy

My after-school remedy
is such a joy for me
put up my leg, relax
hugs and kisses wait for me
as I step in the house comfortably
I smell the food of luxury
as it calls me straight home for tea
then I see my niece with her beautiful smile
then the whole world lights up in denial.

Vanessa Shaw (12)
Hillcrest School & Sixth Form

It Runs!

It runs wild,
It runs fast.
Is it big,
Or is it black?
Maybe lilac, blue,
Or purple too!
Is it me,
Or you?
It's not me,
It must be you!
Is it false,
Or is it true?

Shanaé Dunkley (11)
Hillcrest School & Sixth Form

I Have A Dog!

I have a dog whose teeth are pointed,
and the dog is double-jointed.
He is spotty
and is very dotty.
He is very mad
he is sometimes sad.
He loves honey
and is very funny.
He is sometimes vicious
and I get very suspicious
all because of my dog Tigger.

Shannon Singh (11)
Hillcrest School & Sixth Form

A Traditional English Breakfast

Eggs and bacon, beans and bread
enough to awake me from my bed.

Eggs scrambled, eggs dried
sunny side up or eggs fried.

Bacon fried, bacon grilled
or bacon barbecued.

Beans that are hot, beans that are cold
cook them the way you are told.

Bread that's buttered, bread that's dried
it tastes nice all the time.

Choose your breakfast that you order
eat it all so you can get taller.

Shanice Sadler (12)
Hillcrest School & Sixth Form

What Am I?

I see all the animals like my family
I never leave them unhappy
People say I am the king of the jungle
But I always keep all the food safe
To keep up all the faith
I need everybody to trust me because
People find me scary
I hunt for my food
I am never in a good mood.
What am I?

Sade Mackalae Service & Janeil Amoy Hutchinson (11)
Hillcrest School & Sixth Form

I Have A Cat!

I have a cat who's very fat.
He sits on his mat all day.
He is very lazy
And his name is Daisy,
Because he dreams all day and all night.

He has sharp teeth which are very pointed
And I think he might be double jointed.
He loves rats
So he will eat it like that.

He hates honey
But he is funny.
He loves the wide fields
Because he thinks he is Garfield.

Sunena Sohal (12)
Hillcrest School & Sixth Form

A Giraffe

A tall, spotty giraffe,
whose yellowness was borrowed,
borrowed from quite a few daffodils
with a long neck,
taller than the stars,
even taller than the planets.

The spots are printed thick and bold,
which makes him look so old, old, old,
eating all the leaves,
from all the tall, tall trees.

Bushora Khatun (11)
Hillcrest School & Sixth Form

Eternal Loss

I always thought, how could it be,
That such a blossom, could love a thorn like me,
At first she made me turn a new leaf,
Tried making me forget all my grief!

She stayed by my side through thick and thin,
Through my courage, my moments and even my sin,
I never thought a person could love another so much,
She made me feel wonderful by her sight and her touch.

Now for eternity, I'll never see her face,
Never feel her elegance, love or her grace.
Those tears of blood, for my love I did weep,
As she is gone forever, in her eternal sleep.

I'll never forget her, in my mind she'll never leave,
Remembering her only, every single time I breathe,
I'll never love another, it'll never be the same,
But I know, every time the wind blows,
I'll always hear her name.

Jay Droch (13)
Hodge Hill School

Winter

No leaves on the trees.
No summer days.
No buzzing bees.

But cold, dark nights.
Dull, icy days
And bright gleaming lights.

Leeanne Jade Davis (12)
Hodge Hill School

Winter!

Whirling snow, lovely and white,
It's lovely and bright,
It's time for frostbite.

Diving kids, cool and white,
Laughing and playing all night long,
Rushing along.

Hurrying clouds, fall of snow,
Pretty and soft,
All a nice flow.

Snowmen everywhere,
Big and small,
Most of them are pretty tall.

Stephanie Bryant (12)
Hodge Hill School

Child Abuse

Children walking home from school,
Walking into their house to see a fist,
When the fist goes, the children run to their rooms,
They cry all night looking at their imbedded bruises,
Wishing they were in a fairy tale instead of a horror story,
Scared to tell a single soul.
Walking home again in the evening,
Seeing more fists, getting more bruises, crying the night away,
Then it all ends, it all stops,
It stops before they are grown up,
It stops the day they escape from the horror story
And go into the fairy tale.
The day they die, that's when it stops,
The children will have no future; the children won't see the world,
All they will ever see is the fist, the bruises, the night and Heaven.

Chloe Davies (12)
Hodge Hill School

Celebrate

All our life we celebrate,
The good times we all know,
The fun days out,
The endless laughs,
That make us smile all year.

Those days that come,
That we wait for all year,
They bring us so much joy,
We wake up these days,
And happiness shines our way.

Birthdays, Christmas, Hallowe'en,
Those days that make us hope and dream,
Easter and Bonfire Night too,
Fill us with hope,
And make us love our lives.

So celebrations come our way,
Each and every day,
However weird it may be,
Make the most of these days,
And enjoy the time you have.

Francesca Cox (13)
Hodge Hill School

Lightning

When it is dark at night,
My sister and I always fight
When my family is asleep,
My sister and I always peep.
Every night when there is lightning,
It is very frightening.
Lightning is as fast as a cheetah,
When I hear it, I drink a litre.
That is why I am afraid of lightning.

Haaris Gozal (11)
Hodge Hill School

The Wind

The silent wind swoops around
Up high and on the ground.

It whistles loud
As it swoops around the clouds.

As it blows it moves the trees
And blows all the people and their jeans.

When it whistles
It sounds like screaming.

A bit of wind can be nice
But a bit too much ain't too nice.

The nicest wind is a cool breeze
Because it don't make you freeze.

If I could be one thing
I would be the wind.

Ashleigh Pickering (12)
Hodge Hill School

The English Lesson

He wanders gently like a cloud,
When he is awake he shouts out loud.
The teacher moans, groans and frowns,
She tells him not to make a sound.
In our English lesson there is lots of drama!
She really does not look like a farmer.
She looks like she's as hairy as hair,
Her belly pokes out in the air.
We all stop, stand and stare,
I really wish I was not there.
When I got home I had a shower,
All because of that dreadful hour.

Daryll Lewis (14)
Hodge Hill School

Terrorism Crimes

Don't drive around in fancy cars
Or jewellery from head to toe
Because someone will take it all
And shoot you down and go
They want all your money
They want your fancy car
But the one thing that they really want
Is to stab you in your heart
If at any time you see these people
It is best to look away
Because if you say something you might regret
It might be the last thing you say
There are millions of these people
All around the world
They don't care what they rob
From a car to a lady's purse
If you see one of these people
And they have the same blood as you
I would ask this question
What's the right thing to do?

Dwayne Manning (12)
Hodge Hill School

Bright

Flowers are colourful and bright,
Just like my sister who's full of might,
She's so pretty and yet so cute,
Who never acts like a brute,
I'm hugging my sister with lots of bless,
While looking for the Loch Ness,
I'm out here kissing all the boys,
Just messing - I'm only listening to all the noise,
While this poem has nearly ended,
I'm still trying to get it mended.

Sam Smith
Hodge Hill School

Autumn

Driving down, the wind goes round
whistling and singing
hurrying around

Glowing fire-red, the leaf falls
whirling and twirling
swooping around

Moving left, moving right, white-covered sky
playing and staying
waiting around

Finding birds, playing around and down
chirping and pecking
seeking one another

Covering the sky the fire's purpose is
glazing and blazing
hot fire-red

Drooping down, scattering to the Earth
fading and dying
finding new birth.

Jake McDermott (12)
Hodge Hill School

Hamster

A hamster is very soft and fluffy.
It likes to come out of its cage to play.
It is soft like a fluffy teddy bear.
The fluffy creature is very energetic.
It is very small
Like a cotton ball.
This soft, cute creature likes to store
Food in its cheeks.
This pet is very playful.

Rebecca Tredaway (12)
Hodge Hill School

Parents Are For Life

Losing your parents is terrifying to imagine,
Thinking that they're here forever.
They've always been there for you,
And the last thing you want to happen is to lose them.

To me they're the main people in life,
They're always there to share your problems with.
Sometimes there may be fallings out,
But in the end you always make up.

They will always love you no matter what,
Even if you make the wrong decision.
You should always stick by them too,
As they've brought you up with love and respect.

Never treat them in a bad way,
They're your flesh and blood,
And always will be.

Who are you most close to, your mom or dad?
Whether you're close to your mom, dad or both,
Just remember that they're both your parents and
Remember, parents are for life.

Michelle Bailey (14)
Hodge Hill School

Winter

Winter is here,
the snow is falling,
as the birds are calling.

Everything is quiet, not one sound,
a white cloud of snow
lies on the ground.

Old people stay inside,
children out playing,
faces are as red as roses.

Stephen Harrison (12)
Hodge Hill School

Never Regret Life

Why do people always regret,
About mortgages, pensions, money and debt?
Is it because they're full of meths
Or are thinking about their deaths?

Why do they always seem to hurry
Through their life? They should really worry
About things that matter like their family,
They should live through life happily.

My nan, I really miss so much,
Even though she'd say such and such,
She always told me not to cry
When she talked about when she'd die.

I always knew she was there for me,
Now she's gone, now I see,
The true things in life I won't regret,
About mortgages, pensions, money and debt.

Rachel Ellen (13)
Hodge Hill School

Spring

Rain specks trickling down the glass,
Daffodils growing in the grass.
The house so warm,
Out of the window watching a storm.
We well and truly know,
Spring is here.
The sun comes out, but rain does too,
In the distance a rainbow comes through.
Will anybody find the gold?
All Easter eggs have been sold.
It's Easter time again,
And so we know spring is well and truly here.

Rosie Middleton (13)
Hodge Hill School

Wishing Our Lives Away

Why do we all like to wish our lives away?
We never stop and share each day,
With ones that care and need our help,
We could end up with no scalp.
We never think about becoming old and grey,
I don't ever want to see that day,
When I die because I'm very old,
But hopefully I won't become bald.
If we all thought and stopped to think,
And recognise why we all sink,
And wish that we were never old,
Maybe the world wouldn't be so cold.

Kamaara Natanya Mehay (13)
Hodge Hill School

Winter

The pouring rain,
that crashes against the windowpane.

The icy-cold nights,
that give you a fright.

The snow that is frosty and white,
there is no sun, there is no light.

The ice skates in the ring,
the horrible jumpers that you think ming.

The warmth of the fireplace,
your bright, red, cold face.

The little red robin that sits on a tree,
you could take a picture for free.

Katie Woodhall (13)
Hodge Hill School

Christmas

Christmas is here,
Let's have a beer.
Presents and food,
Will keep you in a good mood.

The white snow,
Makes a glimmering glow.
The joy and happiness in the air,
The decorations make you stand and stare.

The snowman is tall,
And his son is small.
As they wait for that special night
Staring into the firelight.

The night is here,
Let's have another beer,
Because Santa Claus is back,
And if you've been bad you will get a slap.

Sam Smith (13)
Hodge Hill School

In The Fire

I died in my dreams,
not always as it seems,
I died in the fire.

I died in my dreams,
slow and burned by the streams,
the fatal streams of fire.

Before in my life,
I took things for granted,
fate knows I was wrong.

Before in my life,
I took one too many risks,
my fatal mistake.

Daniel Prosser (13)
Hodge Hill School

At School, Like A Fool

At school,
Mrs Pyke treats me like a fool.

Mr Rudge chockslams me for trying to act cool,
Mr Padvis shuts me in the classroom, facing the wall.

Everyone has a laugh, but no fun for me,
I have to go home and get kicked down by my mummy.

I'd practised for my GCSE,
I was told the rest were better than me.

In English everyone got C,
Not me, they gave me a G.

I wish I behaved in Hodge Hill,
My mum wished I could turn out like my bro, Bill.

Sent to school on every birthday,
1 hour's detention every Friday.

This was my life when I was at school,
So that's why everyone treats me like I'm a fool.

Luke Vernon (13)
Hodge Hill School

Winter

The winter's strong breeze,
Whistling wind,
Always brings shivers to your knees.

The snow so white,
Sloppy and slushy,
As day becomes night.

From the sky falls sprinkles of snow,
It's cold,
Be careful of frostbite on your big toe.

Naomi Hylton (13)
Hodge Hill School

Not My Business

They bullied Francis,
Beat him like a sandwich,
They threatened him not to tell,
Or they would beat him and send him to Hell.

Joanne's house was on fire,
No warning, no alarm,
Just one crisp, burnt house.

John's mobile got robbed,
They scared him so much,
That if he told,
His hair would be bald.

And then one morning,
As I sat to eat my biscuit,
A knock on the door,
Froze my hungry hand,
They were waiting for me behind the waving trees.

What business of mine is it,
I am not concerned,
For so long I am not burnt,
Beat or robbed.

Shahzan Zafar (14)
Hodge Hill School

Christmas

Shouting, joy, laughter.
Annoying toys going *bing, bang!*
Lots of laughter and bustling round.

Turkey roasting, *mmmm!*
Happiness in people's souls
The wind makes me shiver.

Smiling, bursting people
Cards filled with money
I love Christmas time.

Limara Dearn (12)
Hodge Hill School

My Life At School

I like awake
Crying at night,
people are horrible
I hide in fright.

I go to school
they pick on me,
I hide away
and wait to see.

When they have gone
I come out,
down my ear
they scream and shout.

When I go home
I sit in bed,
thinking of something
I really dread.

Although I'm at home
I hear their voice,
I don't want to go to school
But I have no choice.

If I could stop it
then I would,
I would ignore them
like I should.

They will never stop
They think it's cool
they should grow up,
I hate school!

Fawn Roberts-Robinson (13)
Hodge Hill School

Not My Business

Dad left early one morning,
almost at the crack of dawn.
Angry with a phone call he had,
forgot to take me to school.
    What business of mine is it?
    So long as they don't wake the baby.

Come home late one night from school,
forgetting to pick up my sister.
Looking at me my mom came in,
wanting to shout and scream.
    What business of mine is it?
    So long as she don't wake the baby.

Zoe came round to give me a hand,
an hour later had a phone call.
She looked, sighed and said her goodbyes,
'She had to go home,' said her dad.
    What business of mine is it?
    So long as she don't wake the baby.

Finally he's home, grumpy dad,
worse than this morning.
Apologised for leaving me to walk to school,
slams the door as he arrives.
    He wakes the baby!

Kerry Bridgewater (15)
Hodge Hill School

I Don't Care!

Come home late from school one night,
I've been messing around with my friends,
I walk in and I feel the surroundings,
They glare at me; I know what's coming.
    Ground me, punish me, do what you may,
    Just let me have my chocolate bar.

I forget to do the washing up,
They've been asking me for hours,
I go upstairs and listen to music,
I get called down into the lounge.
    Ground me, punish me, do what you may,
    Just let me have my chocolate bar.

Me and my brother are arguing,
He hits me in my back,
I get angry and retaliate,
Now he goes off crying.
    Ground me, punish me, do what you may,
    Just let me have my chocolate bar.

I apologise for everything,
All the trouble I have caused,
My mum and dad accept my sorry,
Now everything is back to normal.
    I am off the hook, no punishments for me,
    Just do me a favour, take my chocolate bar,
    I've ate too many!

Zoe Bond (14)
Hodge Hill School

The Next In Line

They name-called Josie,
Threw pens and pencils.
Stuck around waiting,
To start over again.
    Why should it bother me?
    As long as they don't choose me,
    The next in line.

They looked around making sure,
So they could slip a bottle in,
Surrounding anyone who did,
Beating them to the floor.
    Why should it bother me?
    As long as they don't choose me,
    The next in line.

Spraying the walls with graffiti,
Knowing no one would tell,
Cursing words not nice to speak.
    Why should it bother me?
    As long as they don't choose me,
    The next in line.

Walking home, footsteps grew louder.
Surrounding a circle,
I waited for them to begin.
I was indeed the next in line.

Ashley Cottrill (14)
Hodge Hill School

Not My Business

I saw someone get shot last night
The bullet racing towards his chest
The gun smoking, the man gone forever
>What business is it of mine?
>So long as they don't take the life
>Of my family.

I awoke one morning
To the sound of shouting
The police raiding the block where I live for drugs
They killed a man for getting in the way!
>What business is it of mine?
>So long as they don't take the life
>Of my family.

I went out to school one day
Only to find it was gone
No school, no teachers, no lessons
Just the scorched earth where it once stood
>What business is it of mine?
>So long as they don't take the life
>Of my family.

Then one day
I sat at my computer
A knock at my door froze my whole body
They were waiting, waiting for me
For the life of my family and me!

Kellie Cockerill (14)
Hodge Hill School

Not My Business

He continuously raises his voice
Trying to take her bag
I stop and look
But walk on
    What business of mine is it?
    So long as he doesn't come over to me.

'Any spare change?' they say
People stop to give money
He glances up at me
But walk faster
    What business of mine is it?
    So long as he don't ask me.

They push him on the floor
Kicking and punching him
I stop to look
But turn my head
    What business of mine is it?
    So long as they don't touch me.

She runs frantically down the street
With him running behind her
I stop and look back
But take no notice
    What business of mine is it?
    So long as he doesn't chase me.

Kristina Hemmings (14)
Hodge Hill School

Not My Business

One morning they knocked down Monty
Beat him soft like clay
Then stuffed his head down the swirling waters
Of a dirty toilet.

> What business of mine is it?
> As long as they don't start on me.

They came in one lesson
In the middle of the class
Charlie was stabbed then robbed
Of his compact mobile phone.

> What business of mine is it?
> As long as they don't start on me.

Terri went to her desk one day
To find her coursework gone
She cried, wept and ran away
As they ripped up her work.

> What business of mine is it?
> As long as they don't start on me.

In the afternoon I sat ready for lunch
Ready to eat my sandwich
A fist slammed down on my desk
They had come for me.

Ashley Christopher (14)
Hodge Hill School

Not My Business

As I walked towards the bus stop
I saw him arguing with her
Slapping her round the face
Screaming for help

> What business of mine is it?
> So long as they don't take my goods
> My television, my PlayStation, my life

I tried to ignore it
Shelly, my dear friend
Bullying another kid
Ordering sweets and money

> What business of mine is it?
> So long as they don't take my goods
> My television, my PlayStation, my life

The TV I had turned on
'Breaking news - Russian civilians bombed
Children taken hostage
Parents losing all they have'

> What business of mine is it?
> So long as they don't take my goods
> My television, my PlayStation, my life

Then in no time at all
I woke up one morning
To find no television
No game console
No *nothing!*

Blaine Lindsay (14)
Hodge Hill School

Not My Business

They took poor James away,
They beat him soft like clay,
And stuffed him through the jaws
Of a silenced garden shed.

What business of mine is it?
So long as they leave me be.

They came to lesson three,
Scared the class half to death,
And dragged poor Toni out,
Never to return.

What business of mine is it?
So long as they leave me be.

And then Jodie went to lesson five,
To find her seat was gone,
No call, no letter, no notice,
Just a point to the back of the class.

What business of mine is it?
So long as they leave me be.

And then one lesson two
I left to use the toilet,
There was a silent glare
But no one was there
I knew they had come for me.

Spencer Mayes (14)
Hodge Hill School

If I Were On A Desert Island

If I were on a desert island
I would feel like I were in Thailand
Missing my family and friends
Till the very end.

If I were on a desert island
I would feel like I were in Iceland
My computer, my phone, shopping
I would feel I was dropping.

If I were on a desert island
I would feel like I were on an island
All alone, no friends, no animals
Just counting my name in syllables.

But I'm not alone on a desert island
And I don't feel like I'm in Thailand
So here's to my family and friends
I'll be with you to the very end.

Grace Sparkes (14)
Hodge Hill School

A Poem About My Boy

This boy is mine forever
forever it will be
till the day I die
together we shall be
till the end of time
forever and always
he will be mine.
Soon I will pine
together forever is us
no one can pull us apart
he stays in my heart
he's like a dart shot in my heart,
if we were to break up
I'd have a broken heart.

Carly Jones (14)
Hodge Hill School

Hodge Hill

My experience so far,
Of my life at Hodge Hill,
Sometimes it's difficult,
But sometimes it's brill.

The teachers can be great,
So are some of my mates,
I hate the school,
But I like the hall sometimes.

The band are great,
For I am one of them,
The pieces they play are brilliant,
Their songs are great as well.

The lessons are boring,
You can end up snoring,
The water is dirty,
But I never get bullied.

Gary Taylor (13)
Hodge Hill School

My Chip Body

I'm a chip, I've got loads of friends
Fish donner and many more.
I look like a Simpson while the colour's okay.
I'm jolly happy that I lost weight.
At first I was a lumpy, fat potato,
Now I'm a fit chip
I get to swim and fry in a pool of oil, it's lovely and hot.
My cousin, Fries, is too skinny.
He's the mini version of me.
I can get a hairdo, red for ketchup, brown for chilli sauce
And white, which I like to call mayonnaise.
When people look at me, they go, 'I want you.'
It makes me happy that I'm a chippy chip.

Zahid Shaffique (11)
Hodge Hill School

Hodge Hill School

My experience so far,
Of life at Hodge Hill School,
Sometimes it's difficult,
But sometimes it's brill.

I sometimes feel dull,
I sometimes feel excited,
My teachers can be vicious,
Sometimes they're delighted.

I feel small like an ant,
Because of all the big guys.

I have mountains of homework
And many sleepless nights.

But I'm just me.

Danielle Westwood (11)
Hodge Hill School

I'd Like To Be An Apple

I'd like to be an apple
so the sun will shine on me
I'd make friends with other apples
in a new-fashioned way.

I'd grow and grow
and when I'm being eaten
I'll be healthy food
because I'm healthy.

I'd be lazy all day long
I wouldn't have to go to school
I wouldn't be smooth
but I'd have a lovely smell.

James Pate (11)
Hodge Hill School

Girls And Shopping

Girls like shopping for all sorts of things
Make-up, clothes and diamond rings.
Girls go shopping for one purpose only,
They walk around town very slowly.
If you ask a girl what's her favourite thing,
I'm sure she will say shopping and 'bling, bling'
If I was a boy I'd think girls were mad
But what can I say? Boys are just sad!
I'm glad I'm a girl so I can do the special things
Like going shopping for make-up, clothes and diamond rings.

Bianca V Bernard (12)
Hodge Hill School

The Beginning Of The End

Growing in my home, my haven,
Just growing from a tiny bud.
As brothers and sisters grow around me,
Waiting for the sky to cry.

As days go past, they turn to weeks,
Just as I grow, I will soon become a leaf.
The hands on the clock, one minute they turn,
But I wish it to be a week, a month and a year.

Soon winter will come, and no more sun,
The knife of life cutting me and my family down.
To show us the road, the beginning of the end,
Yet we have no way to defend.

Now falling, no longer in my home, my haven,
From my luscious green to a mouldy brown.
Dying, fading away from life,
To be reborn, to start again at the beginning of the end.

Ahmed Wahab (13)
Hodge Hill School

My Car

I start up my car getting ready to go to the bar
but all my mates haven't got a car,
trust me to pick my mates,
the only picking I'll be doing is picking my mates up
and taking them to that bar.

As I drift to get a good swift out of my car
The fast breeze blowing through my hair
I can feel my car vibrating with the speed
all because my friends won't be happy with waiting.
As I take the last corner, my wheels begin to spin
and I have such a collision with that wall
my car parts are waiting to fall.

Sorry lads, I've let you down, now I'm in hospital
with my feet obviously not touching the ground.
If I had only taken it easy I would have been listening
very loud amongst that very crowd.

Now my mom won't be paying
because my dad only does bricklaying.
So here I am lying in bed, hoping to get well instead
of being in this lousy bed
waiting for someone to cure my head.

Brendan Farrell (14)
Hodge Hill School

Custard Cream

I'd like to be a custard cream
because I will be crunchy, creamy and tasty
everyone will like to pick me
and dip me into their tea and eat me.

I'd like to be a custard cream
I will be crunchy, creamy and tasty
everyone will pick me for their tea party
and I will be hearing music and seeing happy faces
looking at me and being ready to eat me.

Marian Zahoor (11)
Hodge Hill School

The Potato

I was growing all nice and peacefully
Then I was rudely disturbed
As I was plucked from my resting place

I began to feel . . . 'royal' . . . as I was picked from the soil
I saw a burst of light
It gave me a fright
But I felt loyal and also royal a little.

As I was born into this world
I went and got a jacket to keep me warm,
Then I was sliced in two,
And smothered in beans and also cheese.

I am devoured nice and slow,
But it is fun down the throat,
As it is like a boat.

Jack Kearney (11)
Hodge Hill School

My Poem

I have a strawberry filling
people look at me all day
I never get away
because people always say,
'What a lovely cake that is.'

I'm delighted to see you
but not when you don't buy me
I'm sad to see people cry
I'm wondering why
Is it because they like me
or do they want something else?

I see happy faces
I'm wondering, *is it me they're looking for?*
I'm so happy that someone's gonna buy me today,
hooray, I'm getting away!

Mark Crawford (11)
Hodge Hill School

Seasons

The snow is forming, winter's near
As the bees buzz round, full of fear.
As snow covers everything in sight
The white, thick fleece looks a Christmas delight.

The brown, bare trees start gathering leaves
As in the air there is a nice, warm breeze,
Bluebells start coming up from the ground
As there is new nature to be found.

Summer's coming, summer's near,
As the water flows over the weir.
People gather on the beach
As a man eats a juicy peach.

Trees turn bare once more
As leaves scatter across the floor.
We are coming to the end of the year
So prepare for the winter and wrap in fur.

Jamie Smith (13)
Hodge Hill School

Just Give Me A Chance

It was the summer of 2001
When all the drama begun
When we first met
I saw you sitting on your step
Broke down crying, a mess

But I will start with your name
Then you told me how your man's playing games,
Your friends told you to give me a chance
I promise to show you romance
Let me in your house and show me how to dance.

Marcus McLaren (14)
Hodge Hill School

The Popping-Up Popcorn

I am a popcorn
I'm lovely and sweet
And I always fill them up
I'm lovely and sweet.
They always stick to my mouth
Because I'm lovely and toffee.

When they bite me
I get a stitch
That's why I'm lovely and sweet
It makes me happy because
I'm lovely and sweet
And that's why I don't have anything to eat
A happy thing to be
I make your heart beat.

If you want a snack, I'm very crunchy
And I think you're like that too.

Demi Measey (11)
Hodge Hill School

Life

People ask me what is life?
Maybe a husband, maybe a wife,
Maybe a house with a child or two,
With cows in the field that you can hear moo.

Life in the city is tough
With lots of people sleeping rough,
Life can be such a daily grind
When jobs are hard to find.

So when people ask you what is life?
Remember how lucky you are just to be alive!

Elizabeth George (13)
Hodge Hill School

Pizza

I'd like to be a pizza
I know you'd want to eat me
I'm thin and crispy
You'd love me

If you're bored of eating the same thing
You can always try my other toppings
So now you'll taste new things
You can always eat my workers that live on me

I'm lovely and crispy
I'm not hard or thick
Once you've had a bite of me
You can't resist

I'm served in a special dish
Which is clean and shiny
People say I'm a nice-looking pizza
That's why I think I'm so special.

Omar Shakir Ahmed (11)
Hodge Hill School

Food

I have a creamy filling
And will go down a treat
I am creamy and bubbly
And delicious to eat
I am scrumptious and light
And I am very attractive
I can make people feel excited
And occasionally I am used for birthday prizes
I am smooth
And have a dark layer
And after you've eaten me slowly
You'll have a dream of me in your slumber.

Sadelle Palmer (11)
Hodge Hill School

Winter

You wake up one morning,
It's blistering cold,
You are tired so you start yawning.

It starts to pelt down with rain,
You can hear it constantly,
On the windowpane.

The wind is at gale force,
For not closing the window,
You feel some remorse.

Your tummy starts to rumble,
The tree on the hill
Falls and starts to tumble.

You make yourself a cup of tea,
Go in the living room
And turn on the TV.

You plan to have a shower,
But you lie down,
And sleep for one hour.

Christopher Smith (11)
Hodge Hill School

Death Is On Your Doorstep!

Stop thinking of you being an adult.
Sorrows are eager to come near you,
But why are *you* calling it?

Old age is going to come,
You can't hide yourself from it.

Remember when old age comes,
Death is going to wait on your . . .

Doorstep!

Gulsanga Khan (12)
Hodge Hill School

Life And Death

What is this life, if it's not fair?
To grow up, be old and lose your hair
I want to tell you all of this now
But maybe I just don't know how

If I was to tell you that you wouldn't die
I would be telling you a pretty big lie
Those fortune-tellers you think are true
They come out of the blue and stand behind you.

They keep on going on and on,
That dark and stormy night they come upon
They force you right into your graves
But yet they think you're slaves

So now I've told you this big, massive story
You might fill the world with lots of glory.

Garry Danks (12)
Hodge Hill School

The Fish

I'm a fish finger
I get smothered in batter
My friends are chips and breadcrumbs too

Some people like me and some do not
I'm good with ketchup and sometimes lemons
That's only with schools.

I once was a fish
Swimming in the river
But now I'm a fish finger

    In a fish shop window!

Ben Wiesner (11)
Hodge Hill School

Winter Days

Snowflakes falling and passing by,
Twirling and tumbling down from the sky.

Cloudy days, windy, wet nights,
Everyone tucked in bed,
No one in sight.

Children ice skating on the ice,
Winter is here,
And it's really nice.

Children going down on the sledge,
Rolling and tumbling,
Down to the edge.

Christmas is near,
Trees are green,
Everyone is having Christmas dreams.

Rukhsar Hussain (11)
Hodge Hill School

Wonderful Winter

Wonderful winter, Jack Frost is back,
Twisting and turning.
Kids waiting to see Santa's sack.

Falling down like hail or rain,
Knowing it's snowing,
But not in Spain.

Wonderful winter over with a dong and a ding
Singing and ringing
'Everyone, it's spring!'

Joshua Walsh (11)
Hodge Hill School

What Is It We Want?

What is it we want?
Is it to be alone or is it to be loved?

Waking up in the morning
with an empty space in your bed
waiting for it to be filled.

Pretending you don't need anyone in your life
so you're lonesome all on your own
no one to keep you alive.

Waiting for the door to knock
and that special someone on the other side
but it's only the postman with your bills.

Or are you saying hello and goodbye
to everyone you meet?

Shaking hands, hugging the people close
and playing games with children.

Greeting people at your door,
everyone welcome, even the postman
who brings gifts and cards.

Knowing everyone's there for you
and you're not lonesome.

Alexandrea Major-Morgan (12)
Hodge Hill School

Summer

Sweating and regretting in your own way
going out and feeling the sway.
Feeling the sun on your face
makes you feel all nice and great.
In your mind you feel glamorous in every way.
That is what summer is,
it's to get a tan enjoying the sun.

James Mathew Williams (11)
Hodge Hill School

The Things I Love

The moon and sun shining and beaming on the land
Making everything stand out.
The way the chocolate melts in my mouth.
The sound of the waves and others too.
Reading and the smell of radiant roses.
Natural flowers with their own wild, beautiful smell.
The sky itself, its gentle touch of movement.
Playing with friends, the way we all laugh
And have lots of fun together.
The taste of fizzy peach water, the bubbles popping on my tongue.
The sound of music, the beats, rhythms and melodies.
My cats, the way they run, fight and play together as they get older.

Makeda O'Garro (11)
Hodge Hill School

Spring

Spring, a wonderful time of year,
every living thing awakening,
people stepping up a gear.
The sunlight so strong gleaming down,
giving all plants strength to survive,
people showing no frown.
There are no clouds in the sky,
birds chirping on treetops,
as spring goes by.
The birds are roaming free,
squirrels looking for food,
as you can see.
Animals all eating as much as they can,
stocking up on food,
trying to survive as long as they can.

Aftar Ali (12)
Hodge Hill School

Alone In The Dark!

Alone in the dark,
The only light you have is a spark,
Seeing no one,
Forgetting about everything you loved,
Thinking to yourself that everyone had gone.

The only light you have is a spark,
Waiting for the moment to come,
When you're alone in the dark,
No one understands how you feel . . .

When . . . you're . . . alone . . . in . . . the . . . dark!

Reiss Monks (11)
Hodge Hill School

These I Have Loved

These I have loved . . .
the golden mile beach in Blackpool,
frozen, cold ice, slippery ice skating,
running down the alley trying to get a strike in bowling,
in the airport looking in the shops,
waiting for hours to get on your plane to your holiday,
Greece, hot and fun,
Turkey, the place to be,
Spain, exciting sandy beaches,
in the town, in the shops
looking around wondering what to buy.
These I have loved.

Hayley Groom (11)
Hodge Hill School

Winter

Dripping noses, sniffles and colds,
Tissues and medicine,
A warm hold.

Frost bites fingers and toes,
Fire and warmth,
When it snows.

Cold weather, icicles and flakes,
Wind and rain,
Iced-over lakes.

Ice skating, skiing and sled,
Hats and scarves.
Noses gone red.

Natasha Sabin (12)
Hodge Hill School

Slice Of Life

Stop and think about your life
It's like cutting bread with a knife
Each slice you cut a year goes by
And the last slice falls when you die.
The knife goes blunt when sadness brings
And then you think of nasty things.
The bread grows mould which means depression
And that will lead to pure aggression
So sharpen your knife and check your bread
And lead a happy life until you are dead!

Danielle Truelove (11)
Hodge Hill School

I Like That Stuff

Topped with bacon
Cheesy sauce
Cauliflower cheese
I like that stuff

Breadcrumbs cover them
Succulent meat is inside them
Chicken nuggets
I like that stuff

Syrup goes on them
Criss-cross patterns
Waffles
I like that stuff

Salt surrounds them
Vinegar goes with them
Fish and chips
I like that stuff

Fat is on it
Crispy that's how I like it
Bacon
I like that stuff

There are lots of types
French people eat it
Cheese
I like that stuff

They are all spiky
Green and yellow
Pineapples
I like that stuff

Birds eat them
Flowers grow from them
Sunflower seeds
I like that stuff

Covered in skin
Yellow and soft
Bananas
I like that stuff

Young Writers - Great Minds From Birmingham

Bananas in my mouth
Waffles in my mouth
Pineapples in my mouth
Cheese in my mouth

I like all that 'stuff'
Stuff, things, items
Food
I like that stuff.

Jack Jones (12)
King Edward VI Five Ways School

William Shakespeare

Young Master Shakespeare - the oldest child of a Stratford
glove-maker.

He *hated* writing, he *hated* reading,
But . . . look where the young chap ended up!
Master Playwright of the King's men.

Henry VI number one was twisted
To make this puny character a weak, pious martyr.
Untruthful as it is, the play was a piece of history.
Well done, good man!

Nobody has written a line to compare
In the last 400 years, they say,
With language so colourful
(Except Newton, with his principia!)

All the comedies, the tragedies, the characters, the emotions,
So brilliant they still read,
To this very day.
(His language dazzles so!)

Pick up Shakespeare and enter a magic world,
In which *every* emotion is explored.
There is something for everyone in this man's works.
(And *always* take in that *language!*).

Amy Ebrey (12)
King Edward VI Five Ways School

Cat Hunt

Waiting in the shadows,
Waiting for the prey.
A mouse would be a delight tonight,
For our tasty tea.
Here comes one crawling cautiously
I am ready to pounce.
Come out! Come out!
Miaow! There's no escape.
Fife's coming, she'll finish you off.
A present for the mistress,
On the kitchen floor.
Then we'll feast on roasted mouse.
Thyme leaves and mint from the garden,
With the head first, then body and tail,
No more remains of Mr Mouse!

Harriet Higgins (11)
King Edward VI Five Ways School

My Brother

I have an annoying little brother.
He drives me up the wall.
He has a devilish, cheeky face
And he always steals my ball.

Bring me my brother here now
I'd knock his face in. *Pow!*
But what would my mother say?
She'd shout at me every day.

Why do I have to live with him?
My little brother.

But I kinda like him, I suppose.
Still, I'll make sure he never knows.

Jack McNougher (11)
King Edward VI Five Ways School

Life As A Pupil

Life as a pupil is extremely tough,
The teachers have it easy.
They always say they have a really tough job,
Try living like we do for a month!

They can call off sick any time they want; when we do it
We have to catch up on work.
And they don't have to worry about homework,
All they have to do is mark a few books.

We always have something on our minds -
Detention tomorrow, the bully outside.
Plus they don't have to change schools,
They don't have to fit in and make friends.

The teachers don't have to take tests,
They've done all that. It's all behind them.
We all have SATs and GCSEs.
Life as a pupil is really unfair!

Joe Miall (11)
King Edward VI Five Ways School

The Monkey

I can see everything from way up here,
Swinging from branch to branch,
Back and forth, side to side, through the jungle trees,
I can follow anyone I choose to follow,
Without them knowing anything about me,
Until I jump upon their back and shock them out of their skin.

They don't know anything about me,
Absolutely nothing at all, I'm totally hidden away,
I almost know what you're thinking,
I think I know what you are going to do next,
I think you are going to change your course and try and lose me.

Jack Betteridge (12)
King Edward VI Five Ways School

Elephants' Minds Are The Best!

Elephants' minds are the best,
From chimpanzees and all the rest.
They remember everything they come across,
They are so tall, they're the boss.

Their legs are just like tree trunks,
They are nearly as wide as children's bunks.
They are grey and tough,
But nowhere near rough!

Their tails are another matter,
I suppose they could be a little flatter.
As they walk they swing and swish,
Maybe it's a swish for every wish.

Inside their brain it must be full,
Some areas are probably dull,
But then again, think what else there is,
Probably enough information to be in showbiz.

Their ears are another story,
Some may think they are gory,
But they are so big and fine,
The Indians think they're from cloud nine.

They are so smart,
They look wonderful in art.
But are they the best?
I wish, I wish!

Jazz O'Mahoney (12)
King Edward VI Five Ways School

Young Writers - Great Minds From Birmingham

Here I Wait

Here I wait, watching you.
Can you see me?
I'm hungry, my children are hungry.
They wait for me, I wait for you.

Here I wait, hearing you.
You think you're safe, you're not.
My stripes hide me: your brown fur does not.
One pounce from me, you're dead.

Here I wait, smelling you.
Your scent wafts in the gentle breeze.
My tongue hangs out, my mouth waters.
You carry on bounding happily.

Here I wait, ready to pounce.
You have no clue.
You come near me; I am hidden in the leaves.
I crouch, ready to spring.

I wait no longer.
You are next to me.
I am hungry.
You try to run.
Too late, I have you.

My children and me are hungry no more.
You are dead and eaten, my deer.

Nicola Quinnen (12)
King Edward VI Five Ways School

Frog

I sit upon my throne of lily,
My voice is but a croak,
Though you may think that I look silly,
You would not dare to give me a poke!

With my insane bulging eyes,
I float upon my boat,
In my mouth I have a surprise,
And I have a green, slimy coat.

In my mouth I have a snake,
Very pink and long,
To those who doubt, it's not a fake,
But very flexible and strong!

As I sit on my lily pad,
Always looking mournful and sad,
Watching with my beady eye . . .
Zip! I have caught a little fly!

As I digest my meal,
I really, really begin to feel,
Bored, waiting for another fly,
Waiting, waiting, waiting . . .

Jack Donaghy (11)
King Edward VI Five Ways School

Why?

Why, when I leave the house, why are you not there?
Are you ill or moving, or just gone away?
I miss you so terribly, tell me why?

Why is it when I need someone to talk to, you are not there?
You left no note; you don't have a bike, tell me where to find you?
My mouth needs to stop trembling, tell me why?

Why do you keep disappearing on me?
I don't have a clue; stop messing with my head, how can I find you?
I'm so worried about you, please will you come back?

Bethany Williams (11)
King Edward VI Five Ways School

My Mind

A mind helps us to achieve great things,
To pass our exams,
To score the winning goal,
And answer that final question.

It gives us expressions,
Happy and sad,
Red and white,
A frown and a smile,

It gives us our personality,
Sporty and cool,
Big and bad,
Small and furry,

A mind is on the inside,
It shows what we look like on the outside,
It does more than we bargained for,
But how come I can't do any of that?

Tom Cryan (12)
King Edward VI Five Ways School

Attack Of The Hair

My hair color afects my brain,
It realy is a goddam pain,
All my grades are reely low,
As I reely do not no
What the teachers are on about,
So I start to screem and start to shout,

Why does my hair affect my brain?
Am I simply going insane?
Yes, I'm blonde and yes I'm thick,
Sumetimes thinking makes me sick,
People tease me 'cause of my hair,
But I try to show that I don't care,
But deep down inside it hurts me so,
Is this the attack of my hair?

Emma McManus (12)
King Edward VI Five Ways School

Intelligent And Stupid Minds Of Others!

There are people in this world
That have great minds
Most times their minds
Work fine

Leonardo Di Vinci, for example
His mind works fabulously
The colour, the art, the work
It has a large amount of accuracy

Wayne Rooney is another one
He always gets a treat
When he gets on the pitch
No one at all can compete

I also want to mention Mr Fox
He always teaches well
Us pupils enjoy his lessons
Because he lets us yell like hell!

These are a few people
Who have great minds
Now I'm going to mention
Two people's minds
That work not at all fine

Disabled people's minds
Do not work well
This is because
Their life is hell!

Saddam Hussein's mind
Is definitely not fine
Killing, hurting people
I don't think that's like mine!

Now I have mentioned
A couple of people's minds
I hope you understand
That all minds are not like mine.

Hasnain Kanani (12)
King Edward VI Five Ways School

Mind Gone Blank

In preparation for my test
I sat, revised and tried my best
To learn some facts I didn't know
It's hard but I am determined though

I work through the night and day
And no longer have time to play
The concentration hurts my brain
I'm on the verge of being insane

Now the dreaded test is here
I sit and shake from too much fear
That maybe I'll forget my facts
And fail these horrific SATs

I look at the test paper in fright
I might not get a question right
I may be the laughing stock of all
And be laughed at by all the school

They'll point and shout that I'm the guy
Who in his SATs didn't try
To answer any of the questions right
Because I was in too much fright

My education may break down
And I won't get to wear the graduation gown
Instead I'll be begging in a train station
All because of my bad education

The pencil is currently in my hand
And I know my mind will go bland
I'll get the worst mark in the school
And I'm sure I'll be laughed at by all

I suppose I will have to sit and hope
That I maybe will be able to cope
With all the difficulties of the test
And try my hardest and try my best.

Rana Wali (13)
King Edward VI Five Ways School

Heads And Tails

Wickets and bails were prepared for the Test,
The umpires stood in their coats,
The penny was tossed and luck did the rest,
The visiting journalists scribbled their notes.

'We lost the toss,' our great captain said,
'We have to field first and it's going to drizzle,
Do your best, my boys, hold your heads,
We'll soon bowl them out and their class will fizzle.'

At least that was what he said as we went to field,
But one hour later their score was plenty,
A four had passed by me as I kneeled,
Four batsmen were out for three hundred and twenty.

When teatime arrived we were all feeling bad,
I had missed several catches and my nerves were in shreds,
We drank our tea quietly and we were feeling sad,
The opponents were shouting and laughing off their heads.

Our first best two batsmen went out to the foe,
It was not long before a loud shout
Our number one batsman had suffered a blow,
A bouncer had caught him and he was knocked out.

Four more wickets fell in quick succession, then it was my turn,
In twenty-three overs we needed one hundred and fifty to win,
I knocked six fours and I was starting to learn,
My nerves were all healed with the cheering and the din.

I never looked back; I just hit the rest,
And then I hit the winning run,
Finally they drew the wickets and bails,
We vanquished the opponents and we won the test match.

No heads or tails
They carried me shoulder-high.

Sohail Hussain (12)
King Edward VI Five Ways School

Frankenstein

I stand up tall and people scurry,
The sight of my face,
Makes people worry,
They try to get rid of me by using their mace.
Reasons for Father making me I am still trying to trace.

He searched the graves,
For the unused body parts,
And so he did save,
Them in pickled onion jars.

He made me strong and he made me big,
From the athletes that he did dig,
And made me a mastermind,
So I could be his personal pride.

But his pride and his experiment,
Made everyone always assume,
Making my life an endless struggle,
Into the deepest pits of doom.

I have the feelings like everyone else,
As I sit and cry,
I wonder why,
The world is against me,
Can't they just accept me
For what I am?

I may look like a monster,
But my heart is made of gold,
I never set out to be ugly,
And I've never hurt a soul.

I am only human.

Vanessa Pollard (12)
King Edward VI Five Ways School

Cancer

I stand in the centre
Of a busy crowd,
Screaming,
My body is searching
For what I am losing,
Life . . .
Is slipping away from me.

I have three months to live,
I am weakening,
Inside,
Calling,
I need help,
My body is fading away,
My mind is going . . .
Going . . .
Going . . .

No one knows me anymore,
My senses are going,
I'm not in control,
I don't know what I'm doing,
Where am I going?

Do they know?
Can they tell?
Will they miss me?
I don't know.

I have to cope
With living my life,
Until I die.

Cancer.

Georgia Ramshaw (12)
King Edward VI Five Ways School

Death Of The Mind

My mind must be muddled,
To make me do, what I am about to do.
It is unknown why,
But it is true I must destruct the world.

I will destroy the love of men,
I will destroy a firm,
I will destroy the minds of men,
At least then I will be dead.

The plane must be crashed,
It is all planned,
I know that now it is too late,
That America will be grieved.

I'm going to the airport now,
To carry out my death,
And that of thousands of others,
My brain surely can't be fed.

But I can't help it, really I cannot,
My mind is telling me so,
That if I want to be free from him,
I must destroy my life.

I'm on the aeroplane now,
My death is about to come,
I really love this country that now,
I'm going to distort.

Goodbye America,
Goodbye my friends,
Goodbye to all the Earth,
I'm sorry so please forgive me
That my mind has been a muddle,
A muddle since birth.

Aly Stone (12)
King Edward VI Five Ways School

A Great Mind!

Churchill was our saviour
Whose great mind led us through,
Hitler had bad behaviour,
And they were blown, through and through.

The Luftwaffe couldn't cope,
Because the Spitfires ruled the sky.
Although Hitler still found hope,
They were going to die.

Rommel was crushed,
In Africa and France,
Germany was pushed,
And Churchill began to dance.

Rhine was their last stronghold,
The Germans fought and fought,
They tried to steal the gold,
To pay for the weapons they had bought.

Joe Razak (12)
King Edward VI Five Ways School

A World In There

The mind is such a wondrous thing,
It can make you talk and even sing.

There are little people living in there,
It's like a library with loads of stairs.

They run around maintaining it,
So you can remember every bit.

They might grow vegetables,
And eat them at the dining tables.

There really is a world in there,
Underneath the dark, brown hair.

Stuart McCarthy (12)
King Edward VI Five Ways School

Athletic But Stupid

I was never that good at school,
I never could understand,
I was good at PE though,
As I never needed a hand.

I never could do anything,
Whether it was add or take-away.
I never did my homework,
As I just wanted to play.

The teachers used to shout at me,
For paying no attention,
They were so annoyed,
So they gave me a detention.

I concentrated on my passion,
Nothing got in my way,
I practised all the time,
Through the night and through the day.

I went through the years,
Staying the same,
No one even liked me,
It really was a pain.

Every year at school,
My grades were really low,
As I failed all my tests,
I had nowhere to go.

At school I was really dumb,
As I look back it's quite funny,
Now I'm a football star,
Making lots of money.

Nik Patel (12)
King Edward VI Five Ways School

Cancer

I was not expecting it,
That I have brain cancer.
It's not curable,
There's no way out
Two months left until I collapse.

When I first heard the news,
I was not expecting it
It came as a bit of a shock
Whether or not I should tell my relatives.

I visit the hospital regularly
It's just like going to school.
I've got lots of support
I really appreciate it.

Now my two months are nearly over,
I'm lying in my bed, thinking
Any time now I'll be dead.
Suddenly, I'm suffocating,
Choking, excluded from the air.

Help!
I'm gone . . .

Now I'm in the sky,
I look upon my family
To guide them through my death
And carry on with their lives,
Hoping that one day, I'll see them again.

Emily Tang (12)
King Edward VI Five Ways School

Torture

What do you use your eyes for
Reading this poem with sight
Looking at the rainbow so beautiful?
I wouldn't know what a rainbow looked like.

I don't have many friends.
I just have Max.
He's always there for me.
As much as my parents have.

Sometimes people ask me what Max is like.
I don't know good old Maxie.
My best friend, I don't know what he is like.
It's living hell for me.

I am really clever and smart,
Best in all the class.
But I'm still made fun of,
As I've always been in the past.

Sometimes I get called crazy,
Just because of my mind,
But then I get really angry,
Because they all have sight.

Some days I really enjoy.
Some, I want to die.
Trapped in a never-ending torture rack,
And it's because, I'm blind.

Samuel Jenkins (12)
King Edward VI Five Ways School

The Butterfly

Bluebell the fairy is crying
As she sits cross-legged on the floor
In her hand, a beautiful butterfly
That will not fly anymore

She marvels at their beauty
As she spread out the delicate wings
And caresses them very carefully
As a mournful lament she sings

'My wonderful, beautiful friend
Why did you have to die?
We had such fun together
When we flew through the azure-blue sky

Fleeting and drifting, all summer long
Visiting bright fragrant flowers
Sitting and basking in the warm sun
Dodging the warm summer showers

Why did I let myself be seen?
I should have taken more care
It was not you but I they sought
It was me they wanted to ensnare

But you gave your life, so that I might be free
And tangled yourself in the net
You made the ultimate sacrifice
And that I will never forget.'

She carried her friend so carefully
And placed her on a petal bed
And covered her gently with a blanket of leaves
The butterfly is dead!

Alice Kinder (12)
King Edward VI Five Ways School

What Is Wrong With Me?

Just because I'm little
Just because I'm small
Doesn't make me different from you all

So I'm in a wheelchair and I can't speak
What is wrong with me, I wonder?
Am I a geek?

I know I am different and know I don't fit in
So why am I not worthy?
I have not committed a sin

I am being punished for my mother's mistakes
Just because she drank and drugged
She twisted my fate

I was supposed to be healthy
I was supposed to be good
I was supposed to be perfect, I understood

That it was up to me to do something
I needed to be heard
I needed to break out and shout to the world

As I got up, the world kicked me down
As I shouted out, I didn't make a sound
I sat there and wondered why

I struck out and grabbed it
I thought I might as well, the world was against me
So I took the pill

I took another and another till the bottle was gone
Oh well, I thought, and then I was
Gone!

Chloe Taylor (12)
King Edward VI Five Ways School

The Girl Who Only Has Herself

He smiles under his breath,
Fluently,
Effortlessly,
The girl smiling,
Covering her pain,
Suffering,
Struggling for every breath she takes,
A girl of only one,
This is all she wants.

He concentrates on everything he hears,
Takes for granted the sounds of . . .
Birds tweeting,
School bell,
His mother's voice,
The girl silent in her own
Trapped
World,
No sounds of laughter,
Tears
Or joy,
But what she wants most is to know what her mother's saying to her,
'I love you!
I'm not going away!'

The girl, isolated from everyone,
Makes up her own way to pass the time,
Her world, where pictures mean everything,
The sounds of her own humming
Is the only way to get rid of the silence, something else to listen to!

Chloe-Jayne Powell (12)
King Edward VI Five Ways School

Foxes

I'm a clever old fox really
As clever as a fox could be
I have a sleek, orange coat
And a long, bushy tail following me.

I'm a sly old fox really
As sly as a fox could be
I sneak around the houses
Ready to pounce on a rubbish bin tea.

I'm a good old fox really
As good as a fox could be
I may have killed some animals
But I'll give up quite easily.

Katy Masters (11)
King Edward VI Five Ways School

Space

Space is logic squashed into molecules of stars and presence.
A second dimension of peace and happiness.
A pathway to hopes and dreams concealed in a box,
Time never passes there, for it is a dreamland matrix.

Space is a place for redeemed souls when they have passed away,
Like no other life before, seeing isn't believing.
When you're in Heaven,
Space could be a key to unlock a weapon capable of
destroying everything.
Space is endless, it stretches on into an eternity of bliss
And you can float on in it forever, needing nothing and nobody.

Elliott Mincher (11)
King Edward VI Five Ways School

Consequences of A 'Quake

It started out harmless enough,
Just a little shake.
But that was a telltale sign,
There was about to be an earthquake.

It seemed so unexpected,
But no, that was not the case.
The warnings had been sent,
No one was able to trace.

The ground was starting to move,
Now in a more vigorous way.
People began to realise,
That this shaking was here to stay.

Panic levels began to rise,
This was more serious than first thought.
The traffic was at a standstill,
'There's no way out, we're caught.'

Soon it all stepped up a level,
Buildings began to shake wildly.
Screams of fear echoed,
And all this had started out mildly.

Clouds of dust emitted,
From the buildings as they fell.
Scattered bodies lay on the floor,
All was living hell!

When finally the rocking ceased,
And everything was still at last,
The damage made itself apparent,
It had all happened so fast.

The land seemed to be so bare,
As if without a soul.
It seems the earthquake had achieved,
Its one and only goal.

Usama Syed (13)
King Edward VI Five Ways School

In The Wood

In the wood I gallop,
Calmly taking the world in
In each stride, a bird;
I crave the rushing
The feeling

In the wood I strut,
As proud as an eagle
My soft mane caressing my side;
I crave the crunching
The feeling

In the wood I neigh,
I am cold, led astray
By the echoes of voices as I run away;
I crave the freedom
The choice

In the wood I walk,
Thinking my captors are gone
Looking for shelter from the rain;
I crave the warmth
My home.

I cannot turn back now
I must go on
Till I am too tired to gallop anymore;
But I can do other things . . .
I can live,
I can breathe,
I can love,
I can be free,
I can believe,
I can be me -
A horse galloping through the fields and the woods.

Cynthia Onyilimba (12)
King Edward VI Five Ways School

What Was He Thinking?

What was He thinking
When He made the Earth?
Maybe it was something to pass the time
Like a crossword or a jigsaw puzzle
Maybe He had it hanging in a room
Like a mobile or a light.

What was He thinking
When He made the animals?
Perhaps He has a special room
Where He makes them with clay
Then adds them to His home-made world
And makes sure they look right.

What was He thinking
When He made the birds?
Maybe He found some spare feathers in a box
And stuck them on so as not to waste them
Maybe fish didn't look right with legs
So He took them off and made the fish swim.

What was He thinking
When He made me?
Perhaps I started off with black hair
Or an extra toe
Or perhaps I wasn't a girl at all
But a beautiful, golden doe.

What was He thinking
When He made all these things?
What was God thinking?

Lara Grew (12)
King Edward VI Five Ways School

Mouse

Who says I'm not clever?
Although I am *small*,
It doesn't mean I'm not brainy,
A super-intelligent individual.
Because I am.
Really.

Who else could creep,
Through the kitchen,
To the cheese
And not wake up the cat?
I can.
Really.

Who else can find your attic
And scurry around.
Tap, tap, tap.
Not getting caught?
Me, I can.
Really.

Of course I am the cleverest animal!
Move over, lion, I'm king of the jungle!
I wonder . . .
Is there a king of vermin?
I could be that!
Really!

Emily Greatrex (11)
King Edward VI Five Ways School

Why I Like Football

I like football
for no reason at all,
I don't play it and I don't always watch it.
I suppose it's just the tension, you don't know what's going
                                        to happen.

You're in suspense.
It is like a cliff-hanger.
Two angry teams charging for victory.
The attackers, a real football addict, a real mud-slider.
Sliding from one end of the pitch to another, tackling using skill.
My best part is just watching the men run around on a pitch.
A real good scorer runs up to the ball and scores, a real point earner.
The other team tries to get him back, unfortunately, the goalkeeper
stands strong.
Nothing's getting in his way!
He is a thick wall, when the ball comes near him it only
bounces back!

Hannah Grace Zaidi-Crosse (12)
Kingsbury School

Pizza Nourishment

Pizza, pizza, it's delicious
When I eat some I turn vicious,
I lick, suck and bite the pan
To get the best tastes I can,
The pizza toppings taste so good,
They taste like pizza toppings should,
The smells give off the best sensation
I take a bite and lose concentration,
Why do I love it so?
The pizza toppings and the freshly cooked dough,
When I cut through the tomato and cheese
I chew it lightly and digest it with ease,
When I've eaten the pizza to the last crumb
I lick my fingers, then my thumb.

David King (13)
Kingsbury School

Rowing

As they wait for the starting signal,
their nerves are growing and growing.
The start is near.

. . . *Bang!* They start fast, their boat is a train
speeding past you through the water.

Their strength is unlimited, the oars are dolphins
jumping in and out of the water.

The pain is building and getting worse at each stroke.

The end is close, the crowd are a group of loud animals
shouting for food.

They push and pull the oars through the water
using every ounce of energy to enhance the forward
thrust of the boat across the line in first position.

The pain is like a growing illness that is never-ending.

They've crossed the line exhausted but happy
because of their achievement.

Sarah Smart (12)
Kingsbury School

Football

Football is great
Football is fun
The time of 90 minutes, all you do is run

Up and down the pitch
Ball going from end to end
One minute you're attacking, the next you'll have to defend.

90 minutes is up
But now it's extra time
A draw is all we've got but that for me is fine.

Phillip Eades
Kingsbury School

Spiders

They're tall, they're small,
They jump, they crawl,
Spiders! Spiders!

They live in the dim
They eat out of the bin
Spiders! Spiders!

They live underground,
Not making a sound
Spiders! Spiders!

They whisper, not talk,
Don't scurry, they stalk,
Spiders! Spiders!

They come so near,
Without any fear,
Spiders! Spiders!

When I sleep at night,
They fight and fight,
Spiders! Spiders!

They spin their web,
All over my bed
Spiders! Spiders!

They're here, they're coming,
I hear them running,
Spiders! Spiders!

Ben Kelly (12)
Kingsbury School

The Creation

God created Heaven
Then He made the Earth
Then came along us
And now this.

We have treated God's creation so poorly
Like it came off our shoe
We pay no respect or gratitude
Look at what we do.

We litter
With famine and thirst and war
We are killing the world so slowly
But soon to be no more.

Why do we do this?
Such a horrid thing.
We can give instead of waste
Still not a care for man nor beast.

We take the world for granted
The Earth will always be
But if we carry on being careless
We will soon be gone. Can't you see?

So stop terrorising
And let everyone live longer
Help the sick, poor and needy
And let the Earth be a better place
Make peace not war!

Kirsty Wood (12)
Kingsbury School

Sporting Dream

When I first swam,
I was like a duck in water.
I swam for my life
I was born to.

As I grew older,
I got even better,
I began to dive
And I would dive
Like a eagle for its prey.

I took part in competitions
Then I had a dream
I wanted the dream to come true.
I wanted to take part in the Olympics.

I worked very hard,
Went swimming every day
My trainer came to me and said
I had an appointment to see the coach in May

I went to see the coach
I was really nervous
I swam like a fish through water
And I got through!

I joined the team
And won races
I was like a swan on a lake
Then it stopped.

I started to lose races
Got kicked off the team
But I did it,
I had lived my dream.

Zoe Peters (12)
Kingsbury School

Tennis

With bags and bottles, out I come
Knees a'knocking, to face the champion
I try to calm my nerves
So I start to practise on my serves

Looking questionably at me, is the umpire
I look at him, his eyes burn like fire
The crowd waits, anticipating
I won the toss, I am serving

'Time,' the umpire screams
Win this match? In my dreams!
The crowd roars, then sit still in their seats
I say to the boy, 'Some balls please.'

I lose the first set, six games to four
I need to up my game a little bit more
What shall I do? Defend or attack?
I think I should just give the ball a mighty smack

I've lost, but I gave him a good match
Where I have been running around, there's a large, dusty patch
I'm going to need more strings
Maybe a new racket and other things

I hope you've enjoyed this poem
I'll win the title some day and that'll show 'em!

Ben Greenway (13)
Kingsbury School

The Gymnast Whose Dream Came True

The girl stood ready for all to see
Watching and waiting she had to be
When she heard the music, she came alive
Jumping and spinning, getting ready to dive.

There she was, just happily prancing
Smiling, turning, she was dancing
She stood ready, here comes a tumble
Suddenly there was a massive rumble

A noise so loud for all to hear
It was everyone starting to cheer
There she was with flexible movements
Everyone could see the huge improvements

She was a dainty and delicate star
Gleaming so bright, we knew she'd go far
She was great at moving to the beat
Then she was twisting her tiny feet

The music stopped, she had a great ending
No one could believe how far she was bending
Everyone clapped, their hands turned red
She was better than what the people had said

Then they announced her fantastic score
When people heard, they started to roar
She got a 10! She won the gold
I'm sure she'll remember this until she is old.

Lisa Bailey (12)
Kingsbury School

My Funny Family

My Auntie May has got a brain like a sieve
She can't remember where the spoons in the kitchen all live,
There are bananas in the freezer and teabags in the jug
A knife in the teapot and the forks in the mug.

My Uncle Fred has ears like cauliflowers
He listens to all the customers even when they chat for hours,
He listens to microscopic creatures from a mile away or more
When ants are whistling and tiny woodlice snore.

My cousin Jack has eyes like a hawk
From where he's standing in London, he can see a worm
                                        in New York,
He can see the rings around Saturn way up in space
Even when the moon pulls a funny face.

My stepsister has got feet that love to dance
She danced from Australia to Birmingham, from Italy to France,
She dances in a dress trimmed in red, amber and green lace
Dad says she looks like some traffic lights and at that it's a disgrace.

My hamster, Chip, has got a ferocious appetite
To watch him gulping down his food is really quite a sight,
He wolfs down sausage and mash and when he is feeling
                                        rather gross
He'll polish off a deep pan pizza and king-sized beans on toast.

Helena Borthwick (12)
Kingsbury School

Me, Myself And I

The air whistles beneath me
For as long as I shall live
The road walks along by the tree
I always aim to give!

My arms reach out to people
I can be tall and strong
I try to be good and civil
And listen to the writer's song!

I am bright and colourful
I am attractive to bees
I like to be different
I am always like no one else, just me, me!

I am the sun shining
As bright as a torch
I give light
And make people scorch!

Natasha O'Neill (12)
Kingsbury School

The One

When I see him, my heart goes into a flutter,
When he holds me, I shiver with happiness,
When we kiss I'm on cloud nine
Whoever invented love is the greatest person in the world because,
I have found the *one!*

Kerri Young (13)
Kingsbury School

Me, Myself And I

As long as I may live
I will always be like this
Forever and ever
Always me.

Like a tree -
I sway in the wind
Autumn to winter
Passes by.

Like a flower -
For roses and pinks
Growing lighter
For the spring.

Just me
Waiting for my special day to come
Tiny bits of snow fall from the sky
Then dawn passes by.

Alison Hughes (11)
Kingsbury School

Swimming Strokes

When you go swimming it works your whole body,
It works your arms and legs,
Your whole body is moving
Gliding through the water feeling great
Doing backstroke and front stroke
The water flowing backwards and forwards
Splashing and kicking in the water
Making your heartbeat go really fast
Then you stop and splash
You zoom through the water like a cheetah does on land.

Stacey Hodgson (12)
Kingsbury School

Football, Football, The Wonderful Game

In the game of football, anything goes,
Famous footballers striking a pose.
The goalie is as hard as a wall,
Defenders are like demons but best of all,
The striker's foot, heavy and hard as a brick,
You might think he can't, but boy, can he kick!

Going through the jungle waiting to get out,
While the crowd all sit there and start to scream and shout.
My face is really intimidating, big and scary,
My arms are muscle, hunky and hairy,
As they run up the field the goalie starts to fear,
Kicking the ball ever so near.

He boots it really hard, I mean the bladder-basher,
And the ball nips past the unfortunate ball-crasher.
We appreciate it the most
When the ball lands in-between the posts,
And crashes into the net,
This is what you get,
                    'Goal!'

Davaine White (13)
Kingsbury School

Failure

Athens 2004, it's all been done
If a gold medal I'd won, what would I have become?

A hero . . . maybe famous
Not shameful, maybe shameless

Palms sweaty, eyes looking up at the sky
Breathe in, breathe out, release a sigh

Weight of my arms bringing me down
Looking around followed by a proper dark frown

Thinking . . . just thinking what it could be,
Staring into dreams, then crashing down to reality

Eyes now drooping . . . looking at my chest
Odour sharp, kind of like lemon zest

Legs shaking as a frightened dog
Turn around, *flash,* from a camera on a tripod

Glory-hunter is all I've been
Failure . . . is the only way I've seen.

Jake Doughty (12)
Kingsbury School

Wedding Day

There's nothing like the feelings
that a wedding day can bring,
there's nothing like the hope and joy
surrounding everything.

Marriage isn't easy
there's a lot of give and take,
as long as they remember
the promises they make.

There's nothing like a special dream
that brings two hearts together,
there's nothing like the bond of love
that's sure to last forever.

When they take the biggest step
they ever will in life,
standing together, making vows,
becoming then man and wife.

Luke Brown (14)
Kingsbury School

My Grandparents' Dog

My best friend is canine
and he belongs to Nan.
He is loyal and obedient
a best friend to 'man'.

I have known him forever
because we are the same.
We share the same birthday
but not the same name.

He is eleven, so am I
born on the same day.
He is my best friend to the end
come what may.

Dale Connolly (11)
Kingsbury School

The Perfect Friend

I have friends who are from school
We never fight, we're always cool.
I have friends on holiday
Even though we're far away.

My next-door neighbours are my friends
We talk and talk, it never ends
I have friends, we talk on the phone
When with them I'm never alone!

I have a friend who lives in Spain
She's in the sun and I'm in the rain
I have a friend locked in my mind
Nice as spice, sweet and kind.

But my perfect friend lives at home
She likes to play 'fetch' and chews a bone
My perfect friend is small and stubby
My one and only, my little puppy.

Natalie Bates (12)
Kingsbury School

That Boy

When I wake up in the morning,
All I can think about is you,
Your name written in permanent pen,
Over my diary in which I drew.

I see you walk past me,
You don't even notice I'm there,
How can I get your attention?
What do you want me to be?

I sit and stare at you,
Your big, blue eyes gleaming,
I can't help but look at you
Your big smile beaming.

Hannah Smith (12)
Kingsbury School

Daydreamer

As I move across the dance floor, stepping to the beat
My heart rate is a volcano, waiting to explode
The only thought in my mind, *who turned on the heat?*
I forget that I'm dancing, think I'm walking down the road

I twist like a spinning top, spinning on the floor
My dress is a twirling whirlwind of blue
Hoping for standing ovations and people crying, 'More!'
But even if the dance is good, it will still never do.

I breathe a sigh of relief when I hear the last note
Then I'm flooded with nerves in the next nail-biting moment
As I wait to see my scores I go and put on my coat
Then return to hear my fate that the judges have sent.

I am filled with happiness as it's announced that I've won gold
Smiling, I make my way to the stage
'Thank you,' I scream then my speech starts to unfold
And some people say that it lasted an age!

Suddenly the bubble bursts in the sky
Nothing is ever what it may seem
I become a hothead, I'm so mad I want to cry
When I realise my talent was all in my dream!

Sophie Cox (12)
Kingsbury School

Upside Down

There's a very strange town
Called Upside Down
Where the children all sit quiet
And the adults make the sound

In the sewers, there are people
In the houses, there are rats
In the alleys, there are dogs
In the kennels, there are cats

In the churches, there are teachers
In the schools, there are priests
In the zoos, are tamed babies
In the roads are wild beasts

They all are vegetarians
They all eat mouldy cheese
They all respect each other
They all say, 'Thank you' and 'Please'

If you're absolutely bonkers
And have nothing else to do
Then Upside Down
Is the only town for you.

Sophie Brown (12)
Kingsbury School

Me

For as long as I live,
I will be as cunning as a fox,
But will be
Cursing the ones that are racist to me.

Like a tree,
As bold as brass,
Growing older and wiser
I begin to rot like grass.

But unlike you,
I smell like a flower
But sometimes I am
Crushed to the ground.

I can become
As similar as the sun,
But when it rains,
I become human again.

Usman Qureshi (11)
Kingsbury School

?

I am a person who wonders why?
Why have I been put on Earth, what is my purpose?
What path should I pick?
I do not know who I am and what I should do.
I am so confused, who am I?
What is my destiny? Why am I here now?
I wonder what is my name
Why am I here?
I must know . . . what is my purpose?

Christina Ly (12)
Kingsbury School

Me

I shall always be myself
and nobody else.
Always me,
forever to be.

A tree
that will be seen
while people walk in-between.
A tree I shall be.

A flower
like a rose
tickling children's toes.
A flower I shall be.

Like the sun
I always shine
for every hour on time.
The sun I shall be.

Vikki Room (11)
Kingsbury School

Sleep Tight!

There he lies, harmless and small
Not yet old enough to be able to crawl.

Rays of summer sunshine light up the crib,
With 'I love Mommy' labelled on his bib.

Eyes fixed on the mobile, that plays a sweet lullaby,
Giving him no reason to cry.

Faces appear overlooking him
As he looks in amazement as they start to grin.

Voices lower as he starts to snore
Lights go out as they close the door.

Karmen Buckerfield (12)
Kingsbury School

When Will They Ever Stop?

The waves crash against the rocks all day.
White foam erupts out forming a volcano.
Pebbles and rocks are carried away in the sea's bed.
Crash! There they go again roaring like a lion.
When will they ever stop?

The mermaids sit against the rocks all day,
Filling the air with the sweet singing voices.
Singing in time with the sea and birds.
Flapping their shiny, scaly fins.
When will they ever stop?

The palm trees sway against the rocks all day,
Causing a gentle, cold breeze.
Coconuts falling, opening up, producing cold, fresh water.
Rainbow-coloured parrots flapping round in the cool, cold breeze.
When will they ever stop?

Paramjot Pagpattan (12)
Kingsbury School

Cycling

One day I wished upon a star
Hoping that my dream would come true,
Then to my surprise one day
I ended up with something new
I took part in competitions
Then I had a dream.
I wanted to cycle in the Olympics
I wanted to be seen!
I'd race across the streets
I'd try to touch the stars
If I could I'd race across Uranus
Jupiter, Saturn or Mars
I want to win a medal
Bronze, silver or gold
And when I die all I want
Is for my story to be told.

Kalesha Palmer (12)
Kingsbury School

Me, Myself And I

For eleven years now I've lived my life,
Strolling along like I couldn't care less.
There's more to this cheery guy,
In fact, the truth's as bad as the end of a life.

I would be an evergreen,
But may be instead ever in pain.
Instead of staying a bright green colour,
I'd start to fade away.

Like a dandelion I'd come and go,
I, slowly dying each day.
Pick me up and I will say,
'The end is coming for you but mine's today.'

Like the sun, I'll rise and set,
I'm slowly approaching the end.
Once again I'll shine then fade,
Like the greatest minds of the greatest age.

Taranuir Mandir (11)
Kingsbury School

What Is Christmas?

Christmas is for games and fun,
For making cakes and the odd bun.
You have a laugh and eat some sweets,
Christmas time is full of treats.
Gifts are under the Christmas tree,
Lots of presents for you and me.
But don't forget what it's all about.
In your mind without a doubt.
Because lots of people do not know,
The meaning of Christmas isn't all gifts and snow.
It's the birthday of Jesus, remember that,
It's not about turkey and getting fat,
It's celebrating life and being with your friends,
That's why in people's hearts Christmas never ends.

Sean Smythe (13)
Kingsbury School

Hallowe'en

My little sister is scared out of her mind
No one knows what we could find . . .
Maybe ghoulies and ghost creatures with fur
This special night is only once a year
Pumpkin-related, scary and funny
I don't think we should introduce the Easter Bunny!

They hunt us for candy and sweets.
Won't accept any veg, fruit or meats.
    Scary and stalking
    Creeping or walking
These weird things come out for one night.
Going from door to door until midnight.

A couple of them fly on brooms
Some of them emerge from graves and tombs.
Their masks are on tight
Clothes and voices just right.
Even though they don't look pretty or neat,
We smile and laugh when they say, 'Trick or treat?'

Rebecca Cooney (12)
Kingsbury School

Football

I kick it with my left, I curl it with my right,
It's made out of leather and it is sparkly white.

I can play on the grass, or on the tarmac,
I turn from the defence and give it a mighty whack.

I can play in my trainers, or in my footy boots,
I play for 90 minutes until the whistle hoots.

I can watch it on the telly, or live from in the stands,
The opponent takes a shot, straight to the keeper's hands.

I play up as a striker, my mates play on the wings,
I go to watch the Villa and everybody sings.

I play on Sunday mornings, kick-off is at ten,
I'm sitting here now, writing this poem with my pen.

I wish I was out playing on the football pitch,
But instead I'm in English, by this weird girl called Titch.

After school I'm gonna go and have a game of footy,
Then go home for a drink and a chip butty.

Dale Baraclough (13)
Kingsbury School

Me, Myself

As the day goes by
The world is moving
And so am I.
Life is moving
Like a car I move
Tiredly I fall
Then fill myself with water.
Like a flower I blossom
Smile like the stars,
Laze like the cows
Eating chocolate bars.
As the world gets older
I go to thin air,
Teardrops fall down
But I'm everywhere.

Shaila Chowdhury (12)
Kingsbury School

Musing

I am incapable of writing a poem,
Because I have no way of knowing,
Whether it exists

It may or it may not,
And I have no idea what
To do if it doesn't

If this poem
Is my imagination,
It is some twisted mind's creation
I'm writing it anyway,
Upon this dark, depressing day.

Edmund van der Molen (14)
Kingsbury School

Missing Home

After two days here,
All alone,
I miss my family,
I want to go home.
Watch my own TV,
Sleep in my own bed,
Hear my mother's shouting,
Drumming through my head.
I miss the family get-togethers,
When we're all crammed in one room,
Hearing my aunts laugh,
Until they pop like a balloon.
The smell of Mom's cooking,
When I come home from school,
The taste is even better,
Enough to make me drool.
I'm going home soon,
To be reunited,
With my fabulous family,
I'm absolutely delighted.
I'm getting tired now,
I need to take a kip,
I hope that when I wake up,
It will be the end of my school trip.

Justine Edwards (12)
Kingsbury School

I Can't Explain

As my life, passes by,
I realise, I don't know why
Why do I always face a day
With work to do and no play?

Like a swallow, diving, swooping,
with delicate wings and no more to do.
A golden light that shines longingly,
but has no place to go.

A single dove, white as pearl,
but has no wings to fly.
A cat, with eyes, killing, willing,
yet no mouse to satisfy.

Like a single wave, lapping urgently,
but no shore to lap,
a single hare, running fast,
yet no place to run.

So here I wonder, why do I?
With no words to say.
A puzzled thought I can't explain,
like a peacock to be vain.

Jessica Donoghue (11)
Kingsbury School

Life

Life is very precious,
No matter what your age
You've got to turn the page
Or start another chapter.
You could live happily ever after.

You cry in laughter
For no reason
When it is a special season
What a silly, silly reason.

Some folk are nice, some folk are smart
So where would you put them in your chart?

A tooth for a tooth,
An eye for an eye,
Sometimes I ask myself, 'Why? Why? Why?'

The Bible is very precious
No matter what your age
You've got to turn the page
Or start another chapter.

Aisha Richards (12)
Kingsbury School

Love

Love,
The world is nothing without love,
Without love you will not laugh or cry,
Love is the reason we have feelings,
Love is the heart's only desire.

Love,
Love is chocolates and flowers,
Love is diamonds and precious things,
Love is pink and red,
Love is strawberry ice cream.

Love,
Love is smiles and happy faces,
Love is Valentine's Day,
Love is Cupid's arrow,
Love is presents all day.

Love,
Love is wedding rings,
Love is wedding bells,
Love is wedding dresses,
Love is being a bride.

This is what I call *love*,
Love from a girl's point of view.

Amena Zameer (12)
Kingsbury School

Grebo Ghost

Drifting smoothly in the air,
Slowly and alone
In the Devil's lair.
Silently whispering
And scarcely seen.
Is this thing
A human being?

Hovering above a person's head
But they won't notice,
Because they're almost dead,
But slowly bends down
And gives them a kiss.
The kiss of death
Draws out their breath.

When was alive
Was horrible, always heard
Until was attacked
By the Devil's bird.
Now when he dropped dead,
The Devil you could see
'Now you belong with me, hee, hee!'

Lauren Wilding (12)
Kingsbury School

Me, Myself And Just I

I have one life,
just like you.
I hide in a small area,
like many or a few.

I stand like a tree
when many are free,
but one thing is,
I've been cut down.

I tilt like a white rose,
and after a month,
I fall right over
never to stand up again.

I fall like rain,
I die like wind,
but once is once
and zero is zero.

Jenny Long (11)
Kingsbury School

Me And Myself

For as long as I live
I hope I shall always be myself
for the rest of my life
until the day I die.

I am like a tree
swaying in the spring
leaves rustling as they
drop high from the tree.

I am like a flower
yellow as the sun
growing higher and higher
till I am finally done.

I am like the rain
dropping from the sky
when the sky is grey
I am down.

Hannah Louise Chaundy (11)
Kingsbury School

Me

Me. myself and I,
It will always be,
No one else,
Just caring me.

If I was to be matched with a tree,
I would win,
I'm not a thorn though,
I'm just me.

If I was to be matched with a flower,
It would take everyone an hour,
I would be a rose,
The red flower.

If I was compared with the sun,
The sun is natural,
The bright, round, orange object,
People would protect.

Just me forever,
I'm not so clever,
It's all over,
Not a thought in the world,
All gone.

Lauren Victoria Romillie (11)
Kingsbury School

Me, Myself And I

Just like me, the sun rises
but I will always be
no other,
but me!

Like the wind I blow a whispering wind
cool and soft with a small breeze,
I help hibernation,
and freeze.

I wonder who I would be
and what would I do
if I just didn't act like me.
I'm glad I'm me, I would never be you.

What flower would I be?
Daffodil, rose or maybe a daisy
I couldn't be you
because you're a pansy!

Who would I be and where would I live
If I really wasn't me?
I wonder and think
and remember what I see,
I wouldn't be anything!

Demi-Louise Milliken (11)
Kingsbury School

Me, Me And Me!

I like music, animals too,
I like chocolate and Winnie the Pooh,
I like DVDs and I play on my bike,
I wear heels and trainers, but I mostly wear Nike.

My leaves are very long,
My roots stay in place,
I stand tall and strong,
But I move in no race.

Every spring I am born,
Every summer I feed,
Every autumn my leaves are torn,
But in winter there's no need
Cos I grow back again from a tiny seed.

Like the sun I rise
Like the wind I blow
Like the snow it dies
Like the river it glows.

Sophie Molloy (11)
Kingsbury School

I Am

Swaying in the breeze
I am the sunlight.
Shining all day
Dawn till dusky night.

Gentle I am
In the spring.
Like a flower that can bloom
It never ever fails neither does it bring doom.

Just like a lion
I am
I can be tough
Eating animals' flesh but I'm not that rough.

I am feminine
A girl - I am.
Gentle and kind
Always having a clever mind.

Isabelle-Rose Tulloch (12)
Kingsbury School

About Me

I will never change
I will stay like this forever.
I will never change
I will just be myself.

Like a bee:
I sway in the wind
all day long
doing absolutely nothing, just swaying.

Like a flower:
growing longer
autumn to winter
never stopping till the spring is down.

Like the sun:
in the morning
till the night
and then till dawn.

Rebeka-Louise Horseman (12)
Kingsbury School

Myself

I am myself
I will never change
For as long as I live
No one will be me.

Like a tree
Swaying in the air from side to side
Rustling in the night
Quiet as the day

Like a flower
Red as a rose
Blossoming in the spring
As sweet as can be

I'm like the sun
High and proud
Always shining
Reaching for the stars.

Azra Amin (11)
Kingsbury School

A Winter's Night

The night, a cloak of darkness
The clouds as black as coal
The wind is howling like a wolf
I yearn to be at home

Watching cars go speeding past
Skidding in the ice
Willing me on my way
As they swerve across the road

Looking at the trees
Covered all in snow
Wondering what they would look like
In the sun's great glow

Now I'm sitting at my window
Snowflakes falling down
Sitting on the sofa
Watching night come around.

Tomas Leighton (13)
Kingsbury School

My Sherbet Lemon Poem

I can see a bright yellow oval shape, like the sun on a tilt,
I can feel the smooth case of the sweet, with little bumps of sugar
sitting on the surface.
The wrapper, crisps lightly as I open it, slowly.
It smells of rich lemons,
It feels as though I'm in a lemon grove,
The smell of sherbet just seeps through the
tiny cracks in the shell.
As I place the sweet in my mouth slowly,
I can taste strong lemons and a sweet tangy taste.
When I bite into the strong outer shell, all of the
sour sherbet pours into my mouth and very slowly
melts away.

Danielle Bow (13)
Park Hall School

I Like . . .

I like . . .
Dairy Milk,
Fish and chips,
And the feel of silk,
My cat Tom,
And my favourite TV programme?
I don't have one!

I like . . .
The feel of the wind in my hair,
A chicken korma curry,
And cuddling a teddy bear,
Biscuits and hot chocolate,
And staying up late!

I like hanging out with my friends,
And having lots of fun that never ends!

Wendy Bold (11)
Park Hall School

Sherbet Lemon

The colour of the sun, the glistening wrapper
reflects all light,
It feels so smooth and it is as light
as a feather.
As the sweet wrapper is torn off,
a soft crinkling sound is heard,
The smell of walking through a lemon grove
in the summer weather.
It tastes so zingy, like sweet and tasty sugar,
There's an explosion in the mouth, as it is crunched
and pieces fly away.
The sour sherbet is sand, dissolving so very slowly
The special sugary sweetness is finished for today.

Sophie Powers (13)
Park Hall School

The Lemon Sherbet

This yellow sticky sweet
Just for me to eat
It's so small and such fun
And bright, like the sun

Smooth like varnished wood
I'd eat it if I could
It's petite and round
The sweetness I have found

You open it to eat
The smell you then greet
Not forgetting the rustling sound.

So now I have the taste
Slimy like thick paste
Next comes the fizzy part
But soon back to the start!

I can't wait for my next sweet,
My mouth, it will again meet
I'll go through all the stages
And fill more poetic pages.

Bethany Gillmore (13)
Park Hall School

Sherbet Lemons

Sherbet lemons are as hard as boulders,
They look like the morning sun rising in summer.
When you undo the wrapper it sounds like the autumn
leaves crunching,
It smells like a forest full of tropical lemons in the Canary Islands.
Sherbet lemons taste like a lovely light lemon,
When I crunch them it sounds like an old mossy tree branch snapping.
The sherbet soon gushes out down your neck,
It tastes like sugar.

Michael Robinson (11)
Park Hall School

A Vision Of Beauty

A sweet on the table,
Glistening like the sun.
Yellow, soft and tasty
That's where all the fun began.

As I pulled back the sparkling wrapper
And pulled away my sweet,
This rounded thing was made so special,
Just for me to eat.

As I smelled this vision of beauty
I was startled by the smell.
A scent so sweet, filled the room,
A scent not familiar to me.

This sweet was gorgeous and tasty,
It filled me with happiness and glee.
I've never tasted a sweet like this,
It was truly a treat to me.

Crack, crunch, crunch!
I'm in the middle of the sweet,
My mouth filled up with flavour
It was something I couldn't believe.

As I swallowed these crunched up pieces
I felt so eager to eat,
Yet another sherbet lemon
A really special sweet.

Melissa Griffin (13)
Park Hall School

What Is A Ghost?

What is a ghost . . . ?
A ghost is a white hologram hovering around the graveyard,
A loud whistle that makes you shiver,
Being cornered in ice-cold snow,
Choking smoke crawling into your lungs!

Ryan Rowland (11)
Park Hall School

Sherbet Lemon Song

As yellow as a post-it note,
A special shiny sweet;
Shaped like a mini boat,
Just for me to eat.

Hard as a boulder,
Smooth as glass,
Almost feeling colder
A dense bit of mass.

Crisp as an autumn leaf,
A fire crackling at night,
Hard like a coral reef
So bright like a light.

A sugary little piece of joy,
It smells so sweet to me,.
Brings happiness to girls and boys
It's so lemony.

Like a fresh lemon, unsour,
With sugar sprinkled on,
I wish I had one every hour
Sweeter than a bon-bon.

Like gravel under a heavy weight,
The crunching lasts for long,
Like the smashing of a plate,
It's sour, sweet and strong.

Nathan Kitsell (13)
Park Hall School

A Sherbet Lemon

Sherbet lemon sitting in a tree,
You taste really bitterly.
In my mouth just sitting there,
Its lemon-sweet taste I cannot share.
I can hear the wrapper crinkling and crackling,
The sherbet bitter taste I'm still battling.
It's as yellow as a flower, as round as a ball,
Its variety of taste I cannot share at all.
When you bite you hear a grind,
Its mysterious find I cannot find.
It tastes sugary, sweet, tangy and smooth,
Its taste really puts me in the groove.
The wrapper giving off a shine
And the taste is mine, mine, *mine!*

Ashley Mann (13)
Park Hall School

Lemon Sherbet

It looks like a golden galleon,
Tossed upon milky white sand.

It feels like a small yellow pebble,
Sitting there still in your hand.

It sounds like crinkly plastic,
When touched it will get louder.

It smells like freshly picked lemons,
It smells like sour white powder.

The sweet itself makes you dribble,
The taste of the lemon makes you shiver.

The sound of the crunching is loud,
The sound of the crunch makes you quiver.

It rebels in one sour last taste,
But the sweet has not gone to waste.

Ashley Jones (11)
Park Hall School

The Sour Sensation

The yellow-tinted wrapper reflects the sun's rays,
Like a sunny beach on a warm summer's day.
The wrapper is twisted at the ends several times
And the inner hard sweet glimmers like the stars in the sky.

The wrapper is creased on the ends either side,
But on the top it is smooth like the stars in the sky.
It is as cold as a frozen water stream
And is as cool as the flow of white suncream.

As the wrapper opens so slowly,
It crackles like an open fire glowing.
It smells like a lovely summer's morning,
Lying in the shade under a lemon tree rustling.

The first taste that the sweet gives to feel
Is a sweet and sour tang like a Chinese meal.
The top smoothes as it starts to dissolve,
Like a nice warm fire except that it is cold.

The sweet breaks down from the pressure of my teeth
And sounds like the chopping of a woodpecker's beak.
The inner flame that burns within the sweet
Is like a fireworks display except a tasty treat.

David-John Somen (13)
Park Hall School

The Sweet

There it was on the table glistening,
Almost winking at me saying, *'Eat me!'*
The wrapper was tightly gripped onto the sweet
Hard and yellow and it crunched like leaves.

I couldn't eat it
Because I couldn't taste or smell anything because of my cold
So, even though it was screaming, *'Eat me!'* I turned away
And left it lying on the table.

Jennine Barton (14)
Park Hall School

 Young Writers - Great Minds From Birmingham

A Lemon Sherbet Poem

The sweet is as yellow as the sun
Sitting in the sky,
Rough and sticky on your fingers
As it passes by.
The noise is like a thunderstorm
As it rustles in the room,
The smell is like a flower
Just about to bloom.
The taste is just like salt,
A lemon in my mouth,
The salt turns to sugar,
Nothing to moan about.
The crunching of the sweet,
Quite an awful noise,
But the goodness of the treat
Enjoyed by girls and boys.

Kurt Andrews (13)
Park Hall School

Sherbet Lemon Poem

I can see the gentle twist of the wrapper
Surrounding the fluorescent sweet,
The wrapper glistening like the sun appearing in a summer sky.
The touch of the wrapper, smooth and crinkled on the outer edge,
Hiding the sweet beneath.
The rustling of the wrapper as the sweet is revealed,
Like the leaves in autumn, crackling against my fingers.
The smell like lemon and sugar, so sweet.
The taste, sweet and sugary, hard and harsh
As it hits the sides of my mouth.
The loud crunch as I bite into the sweet,
The taste now smooth and lemon,
The sherbet hits the back of my throat, sweet and powdery,
Drifting down my throat, the taste fades and leaves my mouth,
For the last time, the wrapper lying crinkled and still.

Grace Harding (13)
Park Hall School

Lemon Sherbets

Lemon sherbets
Crunchy sweet,
Sweet and sour,
Hear the wrapper,
Sticky mouth,
Lemon sherbet sweets.

Lemon sherbets
Fizzing everywhere,
Tasty, yummy,
Fill your tummy,
Crunchy sweet,
Lemon sherbet sweets.

Lemon sherbets
Fun to eat,
It's a tasty sweet
Fizzing everywhere,
Crunchy, sour,
Lemon sherbet sweets.

Caroline Bolding (12)
Park Hall School

Sherbet Lemon

I saw that lemon sherbet glistening in the light,
I stared at it and thought, *should I take a bite?*
As yellow as an egg yolk,
As smooth as glass,
I tried to open it really fast,
It sounded like sausages in a frying pan,
That smell I can remember like zesty lemon trees,
As I bit that hard sweet,
I could hear it crunch in my mouth,
Like footsteps in the snow,
That taste was so delicious,
A true treat for me.

Louise Winston (13)
Park Hall School

The Lemon Sherbet

I look at the lemon sherbet
Resting on my sister's bed,
I really want to take it,
But remember what she said?

'Don't you touch my sweeties,
You annoying little brat,
Or else I'll tell our mum and dad,
You awful little rat!'

I tried not to take it,
But my stomach growled at me.
I take it and unwrap it,
How tasty can it be?

I felt the gorgeous tastes
And they were wonderful,
Fizzing on my tongue,
Tasting unbelievable.

The citrus taste had faded,
Now it turned sweet and cool.
The sizzling sensation
Had made me want to drool.

The gorgeous yellow sweet,
I enjoyed so much had gone,
But surely there were more,
From where the first was from!

Emily Tsontilis (13)
Park Hall School

Lemon Sherbet Poem

Lemon sherbet tastes like a stick of rock,
Every time it gives me a shock,
Most of them are yellow and fizzy,
They always make my tongue go dizzy.

Megan Heath (11)
Park Hall School

Sherbet Lemon

As yellow as the up coming sun,
As yummy as milk from a cow,
I say to my mom, who does hate sweets,
'Please can I eat them now?'

'Eat me, eat me,' it quickly squeals,
'Eat me with delight.'
'But Mommy said I can't eat you!' I scream,
I hide from it with fright.

'She told me you will rot my teeth,
And you'll give me plaque.'
The little sweet glared at me with frightened eyes,
'Your Mommy, silly woman, doesn't know jack!'

'I'm lovely and sweet,' cries the sherbet,
'I'm tangy and smooth as can be.'
I give into temptation quickly as ever
And fall down on my knees.

My mom walks into the room
And screams, 'What have you done?'
I break down in tears to tell her the story,
She tells me to go to my room at once.

Emma Stokes (14)
Park Hall School

A Sherbet Lemon Poem

The sherbet lemon is like a rock,
When I bite into it, it gives me a shock.
All the sherbet comes flowing out,
It is so fizzy I want to shout.
It is so tasty, it tickles my tongue,
I've liked sherbet lemons since I was young.

Bethany Stevens (11)
Park Hall School

The Sweet Lemon Sherbet Poem

I watch the lemon sweet just sitting on the table,
It looks hard and all I want to do is open the wrapper.

I pick up the sweet lightly, I was right it is hard,
I curl my fingers round the sweet lightly and gently.

I slowly undo the wrapper as it makes a leafy, crunchy sound.

I smell the sweet, it smells like lemon and very sweet,
It also feels very sticky.

I'm tempted to put it in my mouth, it tastes very sweet
And like lemon, quite sour,
And I can feel some bits of sherbet swirling round my mouth.

I bite it, it sounds like you've just cracked a really hard conker,
It's got more sour since I bit into it,
It was tasty, I'll definitely have one again.

Chloe Waplington (11)
Park Hall School

Sherbet Lemon

Sherbet lemon, sherbet lemon,
Small, yellow and really mellow
In its crispy candy wrapper.
I wouldn't drop it, it might shatter,
Open your mouth and put it in.
Tastes of lemon and not gin,
It makes your tongue quite dizzy
Now you've got to the middle fizzy, fizzy, fizzy.
Now it's gone,
Ask your mum,
'Can I have another one?'

Laura Solly (13)
Park Hall School

At This Time

People are working
Someone is being murdered
A shop is being robbed
Someone is giving birth
Someone is taking their final breath
I am sitting at a table
People are on the field
Footballers are training for the Premiership
Someone is learning
Someone is starving to death
Someone has been shot
Someone has lost a loved one
Someone is drunk.

Matthew Jacques (13)
Park Hall School

Sherbet Lemons

The sweet is hard, yellow and small,
Oval and bright and mouth-watering.
It feels like rock and the wrapper's crunching like autumn leaves.
Sherbet inside, powdery and sweet,
Lemony, sweet and full of taste.

The sweet is hard, yellow and small,
Oval and bright and mouth-watering.
It feels like rock and the wrapper's crunching like autumn leaves.
Sherbet inside, sugary and sweet,
Lemony, sweet and full of taste.

Lauren Sweeney (11)
Park Hall School

A Sugar Grenade

Yellowy treat
Makes you dribble to your feet
A sugar grenade
That needs dentist's first-aid
A happiness bomb
That taste nice wherever it's from
Oval, hard, stony and smooth
That give you energy so you can move
Painful to bite
But fizzy to taste
Spitting it out would be a waste
It fizzes like sherbet
Because that's what it is
Put it on your tongue and feel the fizz.

Thomas Roff (12)
Park Hall School

My Sweet Sherbet Lemon

I see the colour of a lemon, wrapped so sweetly, wrapped so tight
It looks so nice coloured in a yellow like a light.
It feels smooth and sticky, slowly I unwrap the sweet,
Crinkle, crackle, crinkle.
I stop and place the sweet by my nose, I smell a sweet lemon scent.
In my mouth it goes, suddenly the taste of lemon comes rushing
                                                                to me.
After a while the sweet makes me want it more, so I suck harder.
Unfortunately the sweet gets smaller, so I decide to bite, *crunch!*
A rush of fizzy lemon comes to me which makes my mouth go dizzy.
As the sweet goes my happiness starts to fade.

Rachael Thompson (13)
Park Hall School

About A Sweet

The sweet was yellow like a buttercup in a field,
In the shop it stuck out from all the rest.
As I unravelled it slowly, it sounded like rain.
The smell was wonderful,
It was sweet, with the tiniest hint of lemon.
As I put it in my mouth it tasted sweet.
Then I crunched it in the middle,
The sherbet hit my tongue fast and sour
Like an unexpected roller coaster.

Jade Walker (12)
Park Hall School

Sweet

 S weet, tasty, round, red and it glistened in the light,
 W e unwrapped the sweet and it rustled like crunchy leaves
                                     in the night. It had
 E xotic colours
 E xotic flavours, it was
 T asty and tangy and full of strawberry flavour.

Vicky Burbidge (15)
Park Hall School

Lemon Sweet

I see a golden sweet that is just sitting there
Like a piece of gold gleaming in the sunlight.
It feels like a really hard shield but soft at the same time,
Like it is melting.
As I unwrap the sweet, the wrapper sounds like leaves
Being blown by the wind.
It smells like juicy sweet lemons,
It tastes really dreamy and melts in your mouth,
When you crunch it, it sounds like a big rock cracking.

Stephen Oakley (12)
Park Hall School

The Sweet

It is yellow
As bright as the sun
The sweetness inside
It is wrapped
In shiny plastic
That is crunchy
It is as hard as a stone
The shape of an oval
The smell of a lemon
Rushes the air
Taste of sherbet
Tingles your tongue
It breaks as you bite
Sounds like a hard object
The aftertaste stays in your throat
Sweetness has gone,
Gone to your stomach.

Stacey Browne (14)
Park Hall School

A Yellow Sweet

A yellow sweet,
It's smooth, hard and the shape of a rugby ball,
A yellow sweet,
The wrapper made a fire-crackling sound,
A yellow sweet,
It has the scent of a lemon,
A yellow sweet,
It tastes like the sweetest lemon ever,
A yellow sweet,
It made a snap inside my mouth and then tasted like powder
A yellow sweet.

Jordan Wheeler (12)
Park Hall School

At This Time

At this time . . .
My mum and dad are at work,
A child is being born.

At this time . . .
It is someone's birthday,
Someone is dying.

At this time . . .
My nan is shopping,
Other children are in lessons.

At this time . . .
My classmates are having citizenship,
Someone is driving a car.

At this time . . .
A footballer has scored a goal,
A child
    Is searching
        For food
            In Africa . . .

Catherine Elliot (12)
Park Hall School

Swallowing Sweet

Yellow and like an oval shape with foil wrapping.
Like a slithery snake's belly with sugary sherbet inside
And a yellow topping bright like the sun.
It feels very hard and rustles like piece of paper when it crunches up.
It sounds like something moving in leaves or wind blowing the
                                   branches of trees.
It smells like a yellow, fresh scent, smothered in lemon topping
Or a sweet sherbet inside waiting to be realeased.
It tastes like a lemon but much more mouth watering like
                                   lemon lollipops.
A delicious sherbet sweet, swishing in your mouth.

Ashley Robinson (13)
Park Hall School

At This Time

At this time . . .
A shop is being robbed
Someone is watching TV
Someone is reading
Someone is learning
A volcano is exploding
Someone has scored a goal
Someone has been born
Someone has been forgiven
A planet has been destroyed
People have made friends . . .

Joshua Crawley (12)
Park Hall School

Africa

Africa is a very hot and dry place
With beautiful sunsets
And beaches
Big houses lots of bungalows and space
With big gardens and rivers
And outdoor swimming pools

Africa has got places to fly kites
And bush
Good schools and friendly people
And bus
Lovely camping weather
Even when it rains.

Best of all,
Are the rainbows,
After the hot rain storms,
Thunder and lightning!

Gemma Honey (11)
Park Hall School

My Parcel Of Taste

The bright colour draws my eyes to its hard, crunchy outside.
It sits there like a rugby ball ready to be spun into my mouth.
The excitement grows stronger as I am ready to bite.
I leave the lemony scent and the sweet taste behind,
As I get ready for the sour, strong taste.
The excitement goes as my parcel of taste fades away.

Kristian Bow (12)
Park Hall School

A Humorous Poem

My name is Haroon Rashid
I go to Priestley Smith School,
We have lots of fun,
Especially in the swimming pool.

I am taught by a lot of people,
Mr Malin is the PE teacher,
Science by Mr Harper
He's a man not a creature.

I have English in Room 2
With Mrs Levis who also does art,
Mr Kerr teaches RE
Mr McGonagle plays his part.

Mrs McCall teaches maths
And geography too!
Mrs King teaches FT
Although she's fairly new.

Haroon Rashid (12)
Priestley Smith School

The Move

The move to Perry Beeches,
I was nervous
It's so much bigger,
I have to climb stairs!
The building's not finished -
Nor is the playground.
Primary are so lucky,
That's complete!
Eating dinner with mainstream,
It's busy and quick and noisy.
Horrible buzzers instead of bells.
The classrooms seem huge -
That's good and bad for us.
Nice soft carpets,
Everything is new.

Matthew Horspool (12)
Priestley Smith School

The Bathroom Tap

Drip-drop, drip-drop
Goes the bathroom tap.

Drip-drop, drip-drop
Falling on the bath

Drip-drop, drip-drop
Can you make it stop?

Drip-drop, drip-drop
Someone get a mop!

Robana Begum (12)
Priestley Smith School

Homework

Making mistakes
Mum won't help me
What shall I do?
Shall I lose it?
Dog can eat it.
I know, ask teacher.

Aneeba Ahmed (13)
Priestley Smith School

Feelings

When I feel moody
My face crumples up
But when I'm feeling happy
My insides light up.

When I feel angry
I start to go red,
But then my anger disappears,
When I go to bed.

When I feel sad,
My face droops down,
I need a lot of cheering up,
Maybe even a clown . . .

When I'm feeling joyful
I begin to smile,
I know that I'm glad,
I'm sure I can run a mile.

All these feelings are inside me:
They make me happy, angry, sad.
My feelings are the strangest,
They can really drive me mad!

Muna Abraham (11)
St Albans CE School, Highgate

My Feelings About A Boy

The boy I like is indescribable
I've had feelings for him
Since the first time I can remember . . .
As I got older
My feelings got stronger and stronger,
But now I am eleven
I wonder . . .

I have many feelings for him,
But the question is:
Does he have the same ones for me?
So here I am thinking
Does he like me or he doesn't . . . ?

It would break my heart if he doesn't
If he does, I would be over the moon.
Then one day my questions were answered:
The boy . . . *liked me too!*

Anisa Abdou (11)
St Albans CE School, Highgate

Toothache

Measles, they are horrid,
Mumps are rather bad,
Scarlet fever: dead rough,
But toothache drives you mad.

It takes you, shakes you,
Your face is twice the size,
Your cheeks are all puffy,
And you haven't any eyes.

I would cover it with toffee,
And sticky currant cake,
And for twenty-four hours I would
Sit and watch it ache.

Charlene O'Donnell (11)
St Albans CE School, Highgate

Love

Life's desire for it - love
Of my heart longs for it - love
So sacred, do not break - love
Even better than chocolate - *love!*

Marcia Miles (11)
St Albans CE School, Highgate

Dreams

Dreams are something everybody gets,
There are good ones, bad ones, but sometimes you forget,
Long and short ones too,
And some that make you really need the loo!

Some dreams are fantasy with dragons and giants,
Some are scary with ghosts and ghouls,
Some are strange with unexplainable things,
Some are with action and flying off with a ping!

Dreams can be like watching films in your head,
Dreams are like thoughts while sleeping in bed,
Dreams are for going to after a hard days work,
Dreams dare come into your mind in the day,
Where they stay and lurk.

Dreams can sometimes let you foresee the future,
Which sometimes on you, it can put a lot of pressure,
Dreams can come to you in the day,
It is called daydreaming you know.
Daydreams let you forget about the world
And its foe.

Dreams are strange and mysterious things,
No one can explain them they are just happenings,
Dreams are important and can show your feelings,
Dreams are weird but in a way still normal things!

Nicole Bradley (12)
Stockland Green School

That's What It's Like To Be Ten

Pop music, junk food, going in a mood
that's what it's like to be ten,
Revising for SATs, paper hats and
fluffy pussy cats.

When you're ten, you can build a den, ask your
mum for a pound and blush to the ground,
that's what it's like to be ten.

Pink bubblegum, being a pain in the bum
but just having fun,
Arguing with your little brother, getting told off
by your mother. Oh what's all the bother?

Helping daddy wash the car, going in the sweety jar,
standing on your tippy toes, get a tissue, blow your nose,
that's what it's like to be ten.

Thank God I'm only ten!

Kirsty Johnson (12)
Stockland Green School

My Poem About My Brother

My brother is strong
And shouts at me when I do wrong
He has long, black hair
And a very deep stare.
He cares and shares
And his name is Marlon
He is seven years older than me
And is the oldest child in the family
We have the same mom and dad
And sometimes we fight
When we get mad at each other
But I still always love my brother.

Emma Kigonya (11)
Stockland Green School

Tenacious D

Jack Black and Kyle Gass make this band
They rock so hard they could rule the land,
With their acoustic guitars and microphones too,
They could write a cool song for me and you.
They do a tour nearly every year,
The band that all other bands should fear,
Because their songs could beat anyone
To the top spot, number 1.

And did I mention I'm their number 1 fan
I deserve to be in the Tenacious D clan,
I know all of their songs on my guitar,
I am the biggest fan of course, by far.

Tenacious D, they are the best
They deserve to be two kings
Of the Earth, the sun, the moon and stars,
Jupiter, Pluto, Saturn and Mars!
Now I must go, it's the way it must be
And please remember . . . obey the D!

Scott McNair (11)
Stockland Green School

School's Out

School's out, no more maths
But strawberry milkshake in the café
Play in the park
'Til it gets dark
Going to the shop to buy some sweets
Crisps, chocolate and jelly treats
Sharing with mates
Whilst riding our roller skates
Now we're going on our scooter
Having a race around the lake
Now we are going home
To play on our computer.

Rebecca George (12)
Stockland Green School

The World Goes Round

We live in a world of hope and joy.
But when God looks down
The Earth is like a toy.
Everywhere, anywhere
People are being born
But understand that
People are being torn.
To make this place a happy place
You need to understand
That you one day will pass away
And someone else is born.
But if you're reborn
Into the animal kingdom
People walk by and
They do not know this,
That you were once somebody.

Thomas Parker (11)
Stockland Green School

Van Nistelrooy

V ery good at penalties
A nd never misses
N on-stop playing

N ever stops scoring
 I mpossible for him not to score
S kills he shows amaze me
T ackling is not his speciality
E lectrifies the crowd
 L eaves the defence for dead
R ooney and Ronaldo are his friends
O ver rated as one of the best strikers in the world
O vertakes defenders to score
 Y ou can never be him.

Shem Silvera (12)
Stockland Green School

My Family

My family are crazy
Trust me, they really are.
My mom is always busy with housework and more,
While my dad sits with the remote, checking the football score.
My sister Donna always playing her music loud
Every day a friend comes round.
My other sister, Hayley and me are always getting in a fight
It's guaranteed every night.
There's my Scottish nanny, Nanny Queen
She makes me laugh and is never mean.
My uncles, James and John are really cool
And my cousin Brandon, they all rule.
Also my auntie Kate and cousin Anthony too
I love my family very much, you know it's true.
Now it's time for the second part of my family tree
It is my dad's side of the family.
My nanny Burford, kind and sweet
Always got a cake for a treat.
My auntie Pat, always there to lend a hand
When I've got a project about a different land.
My helpful auntie Viv and uncle Graham too
I love my family and you know it's true.

Gemma Queen (11)
Stockland Green School

Spring

S pring is fun,
P eople go out in spring,
R unning and dancing outside,
 I n spring people sit outside,
N o one stays inside,
G irls and boys like playing outside.

Harpreet Bains (12)
Stockland Green School

Young Writers - Great Minds From Birmingham

My Guardian Angel

Whether there is rain,
Or if I have a pain,
She's always there,
If I feel down
And need a clown
She's always there.
If not straight away
Then maybe in a day
She's always there.
Sometimes she seems so far,
Just like a shining star,
But she's always there,
She's my guardian angel,
My one and only,
She's my *mom*.

Jodie Harrison (13)
Stockland Green School

Fate

My poem is about 'life',
Because isn't it just great?
Don't get me wrong, it is confusing.
Like do you believe in 'fate'?
Well I sure do, cos I believe
That life is too complex
For someone not to sit and wonder
What should happen to Kirsty next?
Well whatever they are, they're doing their job.
Cos I'm kept on my toes.
I feel like they're controlling me,
My family, my friends and my foes.
But there's nothing I can do.
So I'll just have to live.
Even if they're now deciding
What I do and who I'm with . . .

Kirsty Fitzroy (13)
Stockland Green School

The War

I was standing there
In the smoky air
I aimed the musket up in the air
I shot a man on the hill
He came tumbling down the hill
I was trembling in my body
I wish I'd never shot somebody
I knew if I hadn't shot him
I would have died myself
But it was war
War it was indeed.
A terrible thing it is
but I was protecting my country
After the battle the hill floor was red
From the people who'd died.
I hope it won't happen again
With all my heart.

Sam Walker (12)
Stockland Green School

Broken

My blood is dripping on the floor!
The pain is unbearable,
Yet I cut myself more!

Tears of sadness stream down my tainted face!
I hear the voices screaming at me,
'You're nothing but a waste of space!'

I try to talk but who would listen?
I'm a nothing, a nobody,
O how the blood on my blade does glisten!

I have no friends, only enemies!
I don't want my life to be this way, broken!
Will someone come and save me? Please!

Natalie Astle (13)
Stockland Green School

Blue And Black

My mind rests in the clear blue sea,
So calm, so clear, so silent
No one to bother me, space to myself
All I can smell is a heavenly scent.

My problems are fading, though still on my mind
I want them to go away forever
I can't solve them, I have no help
You see, I'm not all that clever.

Thinking of these, my mind changes
Colour blue, turning to colour black.
A drastic change effects my mind
There's no way I can go back.

I'm split in half, blue and black
Calm and dark, quiet and loud
Can't decide how I feel
In the middle of a daunting crowd.

My mind, no sight of blue, all black
Problems have taken over my mind
No way out, mind gone blank
Finding peace, no, I can't find.

Black I've turned to, I've completely changed
No blue any more, my problems *are* solved
Just stuck in the black
I've only just evolved.

Lauren McNair (13)
Stockland Green School

Children Of The Rivers

Summer's heat is soon to fade,
The children of the rivers sing
the songs that they have made,
to welcome all four seasons due,
the song they sing from them to you!

A long-awaited rest deserved
the children of the river serve,
the sun, the moon, the summer heat,
the river slowly comes to feet.

No laughter in the sky no more,
No giggling children that play on the floor.
The autumn leaves have come to stay
but never has it stayed that way.

Soon winter steals our heart and soul,
the world not mended 'tis not whole
all people gone, year after year,
the world will die so soon and severe.

So take our souls,
we belong this way!
While the children of the river play.

Hayley Williams (13)
Stockland Green School

Life And Death

First you start off in the womb, cramped with no way out.
Then you join the world and start to scream and shout!
You then become a toddler that's where it really starts,
And as you're growing older you start to get quite smart.
Walking, talking, moving round, doing what you can,
You grow and grow and grow and then become a man.
You go to work, you get a wife and your kids are all around.
You find that things move faster when you're six foot underground . . .

Aaron Hall (11)
Stockland Green School

The Haunted House

Creeeek! Goes the door
As I enter the damp, dusty hallway,
The wind outside blowing wildly.

I walk along the cold stone floor
My footsteps echoing throughout the house,
The werewolves in the graveyard *ahooo!*

The door seems to have a mind of its own
It slams shut right behind me *slam!*

Slowly, slowly I make my way over to the corner
Picking up an old shovel on the way,
Then out flies a little bat, flying up the stairs.

I run up the stairs, along the narrow hallway
And into the dark, dark bedroom,
Something is stirring in the four-poster.

I pull away the covers, not daring to look,
A zombie sits upright and opens its mouth to speak . . .
I run out of the house all the way home.

And the zombie said, 'I only wanted to know
if you wanted to stay for tea!'

Emily Cotgrave (11)
Stockland Green School

Spring

S is for sunshine that shines once again,
P is for ponds which glow in the sun
R is for rolling down a hot grassy hill
I is for ice cream which melts and will spill
N is for napping, which cats do a lot especially
                    when the weather is hot
G is for games that you go out and play.
    People play games, every day.

Samuel Smith (13)
Stockland Green School

School Days

Children enter the prepared classroom,
They never thought the holidays would end so soon.
Summer blooms have blown away,
Teachers watch the children write,
Children can't wait till they can play.
The home time bell rings a couple of times,
Children stampede out of the class,
Teachers look shocked at how time can fly.

We watch the children play with their friends,
They're all wishing that playtime would never end,
But soon the lesson bell rings,
Pupils start moaning loud,
Their head is now a misery cloud.
Teachers shout and order them to learn,
But none of them want to go,
They all exclaim 'No!'
Teachers give them a threat of a detention,
But they don't care, they enjoy the attention.
The teachers finally get their way,
When they all said, 'If you don't come, you'll have to pay!'
'A detention, a phone call home or no time to play?'
'No' they warned, 'you won't get a holiday!'

Nooralain Shah (11)
Stockland Green School

Love And Hate

I love you, you don't love me,
Life is not fair but that's the way it's going to be,
But I hope in time that you will love me,
And in the meantime, I think we should just be friends.
Maybe . . .

Adam Dugdale (12)
Stockland Green School

The Loo

Today they forecast thunder,
Oh no not lightning too,
I want it to be sunny,
I think I need the loo.

I creep across the hallway,
I finally reach the door,
Flash the lightning got me,
I've fallen on the floor.

I get up on my feet,
And run back to my bed,
The rumbling of thunder starts,
Oh no it's right overhead.

It seems to last forever,
And then the sky turns blue,
I run across the hallway,
And finally get to the loo!

Gemma Towner (11)
Stockland Green School

Night-Time

Time for bed, it's late and dark,
I can't get to sleep, I dream of a shark.
I've tried counting sheep,
Which everyone says,
It never worked, sleep delays.
I look out of my window and count the stars,
I shut my curtains, I hear the cars.
I pull the blankets up over my head,
Falling asleep cuddling Ted.
I wait for my alarm, morning is near,
What will tonight be like? Nothing to fear.

Daniel Westwood (11)
Stockland Green School

Play Time

The bell rings, it's time to play,
Everybody says hooray,
Football's flying everywhere,
Time for a break in the fresh air.

When it's raining, go inside,
Look out the window and wish you where outside,
Then the sun comes out again,
That's when the playing begins again.

Children running all around,
Banging into people on the playground,
Go to the nurse when you fall over,
While other people drink Coca-Cola.

When playing hide-and-seek,
Children never peek,
Children say play time is wicked,
Play time is cool, I like playing catch the ball.

Children go inside when the bell rings,
And wonder what the next lesson brings,
Time for a rest,
Because play time's the best.

Jennifer Cleaver (11)
Stockland Green School

Food!

Doughnuts, pear drops, steaming apple pie
Plum tarts, chocolate, all of which I like to buy.

Ice cream, junk food, bangers and mash
Jelly beans, lemonade, beans and hash.

Custard, strawberries, chocolate covered fudge,
English fry-ups, coconut smudge.

It all boils down to the last favourite of mine,
It's chilli con carne, it's mine, mine, *mine!*

Lily Wood (11)
Stockland Green School

Little Red Car

Little, little, little car,
How I wonder where you are.

Going down the motor way.
You've been driving for one day.

Are your wheels going round?
Is your engine quiet and sound?

Have your headlights got a strong beam?
Is your windscreen nice and clean?

Red car, is it clear ahead?
Red car, is it time for bed?

Don't you need a rest?
In the morning you'll feel your best.

Little car, do you need more fuel?
Little car, you do look cool.

Little car on the road again.
Little car going as fast as Ben.

Little car, you're speeding away,
Little car, bye-bye, you're on your way.

Aaron Wilson (11)
Stockland Green School

The Kidnapped Girl

As I look out of the window at night,
the stars are shining ever so bright.

I wish I was back at home,
instead of in this room all alone.

As I looked into the moon in the sky,
I held up my hand and said, 'I will not die.'

Now I'm in Heaven with no fear at all,
I picture my thinking how I stood brave and tall.

Amy Flaherty (14)
Stockland Green School

Aston Villa

Aston Villa are the best,
Everyone knows we're better than the rest.
We won 2-0
The goal it was a thrill.
We do a drill before the match,
We just about managed to snatch.
Everyone knows we'll win the League,
This means we always take the lead.
We beat them black and blue,
We always buy someone new
It's never happened in the past,
But we know it's not going to last.
We must win it this year,
Or there will be another tear.
We must not be shown up again,
We cannot take the anger or the pain.
Lee Hendrie scored the winning goal,
This means that we've got the gold
We've won at last,
We've beaten the record from the past.

Ben Sutton (11)
Stockland Green School

My First Day At School

I walk in, my head held low
teachers smile and say hello
I turn to my mom and start to cry
I don't want to say bye-bye.

A teacher grabs my hand and says,
'Come on kid, smile, *happy days*.'
The classroom's full of cheerful kids,
I wish my mom would cuddle me quick

School was OK, I enjoyed myself
now I'm back at home, I'm my own *loud* self.

Vicky Allen (14)
Stockland Green School

 Young Writers - Great Minds From Birmingham

Egyptians

Gods for everything
names for things
drawings on walls.
Queens treated well
children as slaves,
Children getting married at nine or eleven.
Men work hard,
ladies do cooking,
getting hot and boiling
no kitchens.
Men tired after work,
Women go to parties
they wear dresses,
The desert is like a sandy place
houses made out of mud.

Intekhab Fatima (11)
Stockland Green School

Aston Villa

David O'Leary is the manager of the greatest team
Winning the match is always their theme
Because Aston Villa are the best
They are better than all the rest
My favourite player is Darius Vassel
He plays football always to Dazzel
Their goalkeeper is Thomas Sorensen
Can he save six? No, he can save a dozen

The captain is Olof Mellberg
He can tackle you like an iceberg
He's the Swedish team captain also
You might want to call him Killer
When you play them, you're playing some confident team
Know you're playing *Aston Villa!*

Adam Atkins (11)
Stockland Green School

What I Did Yesterday

Yesterday in maths
I . . .
Learnt a degree in a triangle.
Yesterday in English
I . . .
Wrote a poem
Yesterday in science
I . . .
Did a practical
Yesterday in RE
I . . .
Learnt about Hinduism
Yesterday in IT
I . . .
Learnt how to make a web page
Yesterday after school
I . . .
Went home
Today
I'm . . .
Doing the same.

Laura West (12)
Stockland Green School

My Dream Car

M y dream car is a Mercedes
Y ou should really have one!

D rives so smoothly
R oars like a Ferrari
E lectronic navigator leads the way
A ll cream luxury
M akes all the other cars look like rubbish

C an't compete with this car
A lways shining new
R ight before you.

Sunny Bhandari (12)
Stockland Green School

Sleepover Party

S leeping over is fun
L aughing is done
E ating sweets
E ating at Pete's
P artying all night
O ff the light, sleep tight
V ery fun it has been
E mily, my sister, is very mean
R ushing in the morning

P illow fights
A llowed to fly our kites
R unning around
T ime to pack up
Y ou got some sweets in your cup.

Hayley Freeman (12)
Stockland Green School

My Staffie

Down the road
Up the park
Can you hear my Staffie bark?

Loyd loves sticks
Loyd loves stones
He plays with a ball and chews on his bone.

Loyd has a tree,
He really likes
He only barks, he doesn't bite.

Down the road, up the park,
Can you hear my Staffie bark?

Jodie Cuffe (13)
Stockland Green School